Difficult Sayings
in the Gospels

Difficult Sayings in the Gospels

Jesus' Use of Overstatement and Hyperbole

Robert H. Stein

Baker Book House
Grand Rapids, Michigan 49506

To Florence and Leroy Thatcher

Contents

Preface

Over the years I have been fascinated by the teachings of Jesus. This fascination has extended not only to the message of Jesus, but also to the method by which he taught. No doubt the latter interest was heightened by the realization that one can never properly understand the message of Jesus without understanding the form in which he presented that message. The result of research into this area was *The Method and Message of Jesus' Teachings* (Philadelphia: Westminster, 1978). One of the particular forms in which Jesus masterly presented his teachings was parables. Dissatisfaction in my search for a basic text in this area as well as my interest in the parables resulted in *An Introduction to the Parables of Jesus* (Philadelphia: Westminster, 1981). One other area in the teachings of Jesus that has been of particular interest is his use of exaggeration. That Jesus used overstatement and hyperbole in his teaching has been acknowledged throughout the history of the church. The degree to which he used it, however, has always been debated. In discussing this form of teaching with my students the question has often come up as to how one can know if a saying of Jesus is an overstatement or not. Throughout the history of the church the main means for determining when Jesus is using exaggeration seems to have been intuition. One simply knew that a particular statement should not be interpreted literally. Generally the intuition of the church has proven useful, but other means are available to help us in this matter. This work is written to provide certain principles or canons by which exaggeration can be detected in the teachings of Jesus. It is hoped that the canons discussed will be useful to readers as they seek to understand the teachings of Jesus.

Within this work I have once again used the forms MATTHEW (or MATT.), Matthew (or Matt.), MARK, Mark, LUKE, and Luke. MATTHEW, MARK, and LUKE are used when the passage being considered is also found in another of the Synoptic Gospels. Usually MATTHEW means that the passage is found in LUKE also, and LUKE means that the passage is found also in MATTHEW; that is, the passage consists of "Q" material. At times, however, MATTHEW and LUKE mean that a parallel is found also in Mark. (The reason MARK is not used in these instances is that the parallel in the other Synoptic Gospel is clearer and more helpful.) As a result we cannot always equate MATTHEW and LUKE with "Q" material. Matthew, Mark, and Luke indicate that the passage under consideration has no parallel in the other Synoptic Gospels.

I would like to take this opportunity to thank Laurie Dirnberger and Aletta Whittaker, the faculty secretaries at Bethel Theological Seminary, for their great assistance in the typing of this manuscript, and Cory Dahl, my teaching assistant, for his help in proofreading and his interaction with me on the various chapters of this manuscript.

Introduction

The age in which we live is properly described as a scientific one. Precision and exactness unknown in all the preceding millennia are our common everyday experience. Only a little over a decade ago the writer was given a very expensive Swiss watch with the usual twenty-one-jewel movement. It is a beautiful piece of machinery and engineering with finely adjusted parts. It possesses a great sentimental value and it keeps good time. In a week it loses (or gains) only a few minutes of time. Today he wears a quartz watch that cost less and has among its features electronic circuitry, an alarm which can be set not only for the time of day but for a specific day (or days) of the week, a stopwatch which can record two separate events to within a hundredth of a second, and an accuracy to within two minutes a year. The precision is impressive. Yet the atomic clock which is the modern-day standard for time is more impressive still. Using as its basis the vibration of the cesium atom (9,192,631,770 times a second), it is accurate to within one second every one thousand years! In medicine today surgery performed by lasers is so exact and so minute that the finest surgical knives of a few years ago appear as clumsy broadswords in comparison. Measurements are now so exact that they are no longer described in fractions of an inch or millimeter. The present standard is the wavelength of krypton 86 (1,650,763.73 per meter), and with the use of the laser we can now measure to a precision of a ten-millionth of an inch. No longer do we depend on the pendulum, gears, springs, or the yardstick for measurement, but we now depend instead on wavelengths and vibrations of atoms!

As a result of scientific advance, our culture is permeated with the desire and demand for accuracy and precision. This demand seeks to discover even more exact and finer yard-sticks. The biblical world, by contrast, was a prescientific one. It had not the ability, the need, nor the desire for such accuracy. It was not concerned with distinguishing between fine shades of blue or various hues of red but with dis-tinguishing between black and white. Its timepiece was the sun; its measuring device a cubit rod or a day's journey. In light of all this it is sometimes difficult for present-day believers to identify with the Bible because the Bible is pre-scientific. This does not mean that it is antiscientific, but simply that it is ascientific. It was written by people who were inspired but who were nonetheless unacquainted with the scientific values and abilities of our day and age. It was written by people who loved picturesque language, riddles, and analogies. They were a people who loved to exaggerate and tell stories.[1] What T. E. Lawrence said about the Arabs he worked with in the second decade of our century could probably be said also of the people of the Bible:

> In the very outset, at the first meeting with them, was found a universal clearness or hardness of belief, almost mathematical in its limitation, and repellent in its unsym-pathetic form. Semites had no half-tones in their register of vision. They were a people of primary colours, or rather of black and white, who saw the world always in contour. They were a dogmatic people, despising doubt, our modern crown of thorns. They did not understand our metaphysical difficulties, our introspective questionings. They knew only truth and untruth, belief and unbelief, without our hesitating retinue of finer shades.
>
> This people was black and white, not only in vision, but by inmost furnishing: black and white not merely in clarity, but in apposition. Their thoughts were at ease only in extremes. They inhabited superlatives by choice.[2]

The canonical writers clearly used exaggeration more than

did their contemporaries; in fact, "no Greek or Roman writer of antiquity equals the writers of the Old and the New Testaments in the use of exaggeration."[3] (Using the language of structuralism we might say that the biblical writers were especially fond of binary relations or binary sets.)

Yet exaggeration is not merely a prescientific phenomenon. It is present in our own culture as well. When a young man writes his sweetheart that in her presence his heart skips a beat and the stars sparkle more brightly, he is clearly exaggerating. Even if he is a cardiologist or an astronomer, in this context he eschews scientific precision for the hyperbolic language of lovers. The size of a fish is most likely to be exaggerated, even when it is reported by an engineer in the Bureau of Measurements; in describing his grandchildren a child psychiatrist is less likely to offer a precise psychiatric analysis than an exaggerated comment of a proud grandfather! In baseball we speak of a batter's having hit the ball a mile (or, to mix metaphors, having hit it a ton). In football we speak of pinpoint passing or kicking the ball out of the stadium. To unexpected guests who drop by we say that putting them up for the night is absolutely no trouble at all, even though we must run around the house to make arrangements. For the good student, flunking or "bombing" an exam may mean that he will receive only a B. The concert pianist who has given a poor performance may claim that he made a million mistakes. And when it comes to advertisements, who today does not believe that what is said is grossly exaggerated at best!

In communication of any kind one must be aware of the genre. Exaggeration is permissible and probably expected in fish stories, but not in automobile-repair manuals. The fish can be described as at least three feet long, but the spark-plug gap must be exactly 0.016 of an inch. Instantly and perhaps unconsciously we recognize that the fish story and the repair manual are two different genres, and we adjust our thinking accordingly. To further illustrate this point, we present here two separate pieces of correspondence.

Both are written by the same individual. Note how unconsciously and intuitively we adjust our approach to each of them.

July 21, 1985

My dearest Joan,

These last few days that we have been apart have been the loneliest days of my life. I have not slept a wink since you returned home. I cannot eat; my studies are meaningless; I cannot get any work done; and I cannot think about anything but you. I feel that life has become meaningless when we are apart, and without you I would rather be dead. I cannot wait until we are together again, for only then will my heart begin to beat once more. I shall hold my breath until I see you this weekend.

With all my love,
Bob

July 21, 1985

Dear Dr. Anderson:

I have examined Mr. Smith, whom you referred to me for cardiac evaluation because of his complaint of palpitations. On clinical exam he has a mid-systolic murmur preceded by an early to mid-systolic click. Occasional dropped beats occurred also. Electrocardiogram revealed no abnormalities other than occasional atrial tachycardia. An echocardiogram was also performed. Definite evidence of a prolapsing or "floppy" mitral valve leaflet was found. With this evidence I believe that Mr. Smith's palpitations are due to paroxysmal atrial tachycardia related to his prolapsing mitral valve.

Sincerely yours,
Dr. Robert H. Stone

Here we have two examples of correspondence by Dr. Robert H. Stone, an intern in cardiology. The first is a love letter to his sweetheart. The same day he wrote a note to another physician concerning the diagnosis of a patient. It is evident that we have in these two writings two different genres which require different methods of interpretation, that is, different hermeneutics; for if we were to read both writings in the same way, one of them would of necessity be misunderstood. The medical report is to be read literally. There is no exaggeration present; each line is to be read and interpreted as an exact scientific description of the physical condition of the patient. The purpose is to reveal precise cognitive information about the patient and his heart condition. The first letter, however, does not contain a single sentence that can be interpreted literally. Dr. Stone's heart has not skipped a single beat since he bade farewell to his beloved (literally, he does not have paroxysmal atrial tachycardia). He has, of course, been breathing regularly. Whatever may be his sleeping, eating, study, and work habits, it is certain that he has continued in all these activities. The medical analysis reveals that he is still very much involved in his work. Yet the recipient of Dr. Stone's love letter knows this, for she is aware that in love letters all sorts of exaggeration are not only permitted but expected. She realizes intuitively that the purpose of such a letter is not merely to reveal certain information but also to affect her emotions, and that this can be done far more effectively by the use of exaggerated and picturesque language. The second letter, on the other hand, purposely seeks to avoid all emotions and feelings in order to convey certain information with regard to Mr. Smith's heart.

In our discussion of exaggeration in the teachings of Jesus, we shall seek to do three things. In chapter 1 we will seek to establish that exaggeration is indeed present in the teachings of Jesus. We shall not seek in this work, however, to determine whether the various sayings of Jesus which are discussed are authentic. Rather we shall seek only to establish that certain sayings attributed to Jesus in the Gospels contain exaggeration. We shall leave to the reader the task of determining to what *Sitz im Leben* the individual sayings actually belong. Note, furthermore, that we have not entitled this work *Exaggeration in the Gospels*, because we shall not deal with exaggeration in the narratives in which these sayings of Jesus are found, nor with the overstatements of John the Baptist and others. In chapter 2 we shall seek to establish certain principles or guidelines for recognizing the presence of exaggeration in the teachings of Jesus (and in other literature as well). Finally, in chapter 3 we shall discuss the various purposes of exaggeration. With this knowledge we shall be better able to determine how Jesus' original audience would have reacted and how we today should understand and respond to such sayings.

It should be pointed out that recognizing literary devices in the biblical materials is not the same as treating the Bible purely as literature. Our aim lies far beyond reading the Bible purely as literature, far beyond the pursuit of literary insight and enjoyment, for it is not possible to respond to the message and challenge of Jesus simply by understanding its literary form. The proper response to MARK 8:35 ("For whoever would save his life will lose it; and whoever loses his life for my sake and the gospel's will save it") is not recognition that the form of this saying is antithetical parallelism. Nor is the proper response to LUKE 14:26 ("If any one comes to me and does not hate his own father and mother and wife and children and brothers and sisters, yes, and even his own life, he cannot be my disciple") that we have here an example of overstatement. Surely a confrontation with the message of Jesus demands obedience rather than scholarly description, submission rather than mere literary definition! For those who see in the Bible the Word of God, it is impossible to treat the Bible with antiseptic objectivity as mere literature. For the Christian "it is almost fantastic to suppose that one might read [the Bible] without recognizing that it was written not out of joy in the sonorousness of its own language, out of pleasure in its own literary quality, but because it wanted to say something about God and his works, God and his dealings with man."[4] Therefore, our discussion of the exaggerated nature of certain sayings of Jesus should not be construed as suggesting that recognition of various passages as overstatement or hyperbole is an end in itself. Rather, this is only one step in the entire hermeneutical process. Our purpose in developing an ability to recognize and understand exaggeration is to hear the message of Jesus (and the Evangelists) more clearly. Our goal is to understand more plainly what

Jesus meant by these words and what their significance is for us today. Unless we come to this point in our investigation of the teachings of Jesus, all our efforts and research will be a mere exercise in literary criticism and will profit us little, for we shall not have heard the Word of God.

Notes

1. Stephen J. Brown, *Image and Truth: Studies in the Imagery of the Bible* (Rome: Catholic Book Agency, 1955), pp. 45–46, summarizes this tendency: "The Oriental imagination delights in simile, metaphor, allegory, hyperbole and a hundred other figures."

2. T. E. Lawrence, *Seven Pillars of Wisdom* (New York: Doubleday, 1953), p. 38.

3. Claude C. Douglas, *Overstatement in the New Testament* (New York: Henry Holt, 1931), p. xxi.

4. James Barr, "Reading the Bible as Literature," *Bulletin of the John Rylands University Library of Manchester* 56 (1973): 15.

1

Exaggeration in the Teachings of Jesus

Within the four canonical Gospels we find numerous occasions of exaggeration on the lips of Jesus. At times the exaggeration is hyperbolic in that what is commanded or portrayed is literally impossible or inconceivable. At other times the exaggeration is more of an overstatement in that what is commanded or portrayed is possible or conceivable, but a literal fulfilment or enactment would be contrary to the intention of Jesus. For our purpose this distinction between hyperbole and overstatement is of no major importance since both are forms of exaggeration in the teachings of Jesus.

Perhaps the clearest way in which we can see Jesus' use of exaggeration is to place side by side, to the degree that this is possible, examples of exaggeration and literal statements which are related in theme.

Why do you see the speck that is in your brother's eye, but do not notice the log that is in your own eye? Or how can you say to your brother, "Let me take the speck out of your eye," when there is the log in your own eye? You hypocrite, first take the

If your brother sins against you, go and tell him his fault, between you and him alone. If he listens to you, you have gained your brother. But if he does not listen, take one or two others along with you, that every word may be confirmed by

log out of your own eye, and then you will see clearly to take the speck out of your brother's eye. [MATT. 7:3-5]	the evidence of two or three witnesses. If he refuses to listen to them, tell it to the church; and if he refuses to listen even to the church, let him be to you as a Gentile and a tax collector. [Matt. 18:15-17]

The saying found in Matthew 18:15-17 has frequently been seen as being nonauthentic due to its proleptic reference to the church. This assumption can be debated. But even if this were a saying that came to the Evangelist not so much from the historical Jesus as from the risen Christ, it nevertheless demonstrates by its more literal character the exaggerated nature of MATTHEW 7:3-5. The saying in Matthew 18:15-17 is not meant to be understood as an exaggeration. On the contrary, there is provided here a clear step-by-step procedure that the individual is to follow in the community of faith. Far from being impossible (hyperbolic), the procedure by which a wronged believer is to seek reconciliation with his fellow believer ("brother") seemed quite obvious to the leaders of the early church, for in their commentaries on this passage we find little or no allegorical interpretation. The words were understood and applied quite literally.[1] On the other hand, the impossibility of carrying out MATTHEW 7:3-5 and the existence here of hyperbolic language are immediately evident. Logs simply cannot fit in human eyes! The image is indeed powerful and impressive, but it is not at all literal. Its very exaggeration forcefully confronts the hearer with the demand of Jesus.

With regard to the need of repentance as a requirement for entering the kingdom of God we can compare the following statements:

If your right eye causes you to sin, pluck it out and throw it away; it is better that you lose one of your members than that your whole body	There were some present at that very time who told him of the Galileans whose blood Pilate had mingled with their sacrifices. And [Jesus] an-

be thrown into hell. And if your right hand causes you to sin, cut it off and throw it away; it is better that you lose one of your members than that your whole body go into hell. [MATT. 5:29-30]

swered them, "Do you think that these Galileans were worse sinners than all the other Galileans, because they suffered thus? I tell you, No; but unless you repent you will all likewise perish. Or those eighteen upon whom the tower in Siloam fell and killed them, do you think that they were worse offenders than all the others who dwelt in Jerusalem? I tell you, No; but unless you repent you will all likewise perish." [Luke 13:1-5]

In MATTHEW 5:29-30 the act of turning away from sin is portrayed as the plucking out of one's right eye or the cutting off of one's right hand. That the saying is an example of overstatement (exaggeration which is literally possible) rather than hyperbole (exaggeration which is literally impossible) is evident from the tragic fact that in the history of the church these words have on occasion been literally carried out! Yet certainly Jesus did not intend a literal observance of his words, for the removal of the right eye does not prohibit the left eye from continuing to look lustfully. Even the removal of both eyes cannot prohibit lust! Such self-mutilation was not practiced by those who heard Jesus, for they knew that the language he used was meant to effect change and impress upon them the need to repent rather than to describe literally how repentance is to be carried out. On the other hand, the commands to repent in Luke 13:3 and 5 were and are to be understood as literal commands, for Jesus continually preached, "Repent, for the kingdom of heaven is at hand" (MATT. 4:17).

In the Sermon on the Mount we find placed next to each other sayings on prayer that are in one instance exaggerated and in the other quite literal:

And when you pray, you must not be like the hypocrites; for they love to stand and pray in the synagogues and at the street corners, that they may be seen by men. Truly, I say to you, they have their reward. But when you pray, go into your room and shut the door and pray to your Father who is in secret; and your Father who sees in secret will reward you. [Matt. 6:5–6]

And in praying do not heap up empty phrases as the Gentiles do; for they think that they will be heard for their many words. Do not be like them, for your Father knows what you need before you ask him. Pray then like this:

Our Father who art in
   heaven,
Hallowed be thy name.
Thy kingdom come,
Thy will be done,
   On earth as it is in
     heaven.
Give us this day our daily
   bread;
And forgive us our debts,
   As we also have
     forgiven our debtors;
And lead us not into
   temptation,
   But deliver us from evil.
[MATT. 6:7–13]

In reacting to the practice of certain hypocrites who prayed both in church (literally, the synagogue) as well as in public places in order to appear as devout and pious men, Jesus tells his followers that true prayer is not a performance for others to see. He remarks ironically that those who pray in this manner have already received their due. The only thing their prayer achieves is recognition by others that they are praying and that they are, supposedly, devout men. God, however, ignores such prayer! Jesus' followers are to pray not in order to be seen by others, but in order to be heard by God. They are therefore to pray in their inner room (probably the storeroom of their home) with the door shut. Then, although unnoticed by men, their prayers will be heard by God. Every Jew who heard Jesus say these words would have known immediately that this statement is an exaggeration. They knew that at both the synagogue and temple there were times of corporate prayer in which they were to take part, and they also knew that they could pray to God anywhere at any time. They had, furthermore, seen Jesus pray—both privately (MATT. 14:23) and publicly (MATT. 19:13)—on occasions when he was not in an inner room.

The teachings on prayer in MATTHEW 6:7–13, on the other hand, are quite literal in character, and, indeed, the church from its inception used the Lord's Prayer corporately in worship. Note the first-person plurals in this prayer: they reveal clearly that the prayer is not to be uttered privately in one's room but corporately with other believers. These plurals are also found in the Lukan version of the prayer (cf. LUKE 11:2–4). It is quite clear, therefore, that Jesus' words about praying in private in one's inner room, given as they were in reaction to the hypocritical practice of some religious leaders, were intended to be an impressionistic portrayal of the kind of prayer that is acceptable before God; they were not meant to be taken as a literal command that his followers should pray only behind closed doors. No, the point Jesus was making was that personal prayer is not to be a stage performance for the sake of an audience and their adulation, but rather is to be a private communion with the Father.

Two declaratory statements regarding the future likewise exemplify the difference between a literal and an exaggerated remark:

And Jesus said to him, "Do you see these great buildings? There will not be left here one stone upon another, that will not be thrown down." [MARK 13:2]

Nothing is covered up that will not be revealed, or hidden that will not be known. [LUKE 12:2]

In Jesus' statement that one day all things will be made manifest, nothing remaining secret, we have a confession of a general Jewish belief and principle, for Jesus' audience readily agreed that the day will come when God, who knows the secrets in the hearts of all people (Ps. 139; Dan. 2:20–23, 27–30), will judge the world. This both Jesus and his audience believed would literally take place. As for the saying concerning the great buildings of Jerusalem, doubtless most would agree that the horrors of A.D. 70 when the Roman armies under Titus destroyed Jerusalem fulfilled these words. The destruction was so massive and extensive that the Tyropoeon Valley simply disappeared as it was filled in with the rubble of the city, the temple, and the temple mount. Yet even today one can see in Jerusalem at the Wailing Wall of the temple mount some of the very courses of Herodian foundation stones to which Jesus referred. Not all of the stones were separated from each other. Some stones even today remain upon each other! MARK 13:2 has not, then, been literally fulfilled. Yet surely no one would deny that the meaning of the words of Jesus was indeed fulfilled in a most horrible way in A.D. 70. MARK 13:2 is an impressionistic saying which uses exaggeration in order to depict in a vivid manner the temporalness of all human monuments and the horror of the destruction that Jerusalem would soon experience. (If an individual were to state that on January 15, ten years from now, an earthquake will destroy the Empire State Building, so that not a single brick will remain attached to another, and if on that very day an earthquake does occur and the Empire State Building collapses into a huge heap of rubble, certainly no one would claim that the prediction has not actually been fulfilled simply because two bricks still cemented together might be found lying in the rubble!)

Within the Sermon on the Mount there are a number of sayings which deal with the subject of forgiveness. Two of them illustrate once again the difference between a statement which is to be interpreted literally and one which is to be understood as using exaggeration:

| So if you are offering your gift at the altar, and there remember that your brother | For if you forgive men their trespasses, your heavenly Father also will forgive you; |

has something against you, leave your gift there before the altar and go; first be reconciled to your brother, and then come and offer your gift. [Matt. 5:23-24]

but if you do not forgive men their trespasses, neither will your Father forgive your trespasses. [Matt. 6:14-15]

In the first of the six antitheses of the Sermon on the Mount ("You have heard that it was said . . . but I say to you . . .") Jesus deals with the subject of murder and anger. In light of Matthew 5:17-20 it is clear that Jesus here does not reject but intensifies the Old Testament commandment concerning killing (Exod. 20:13): he includes in this commandment prohibition of anger and hatred as well as murder. The believer is always to seek reconciliation with his fellow believer (literally, brother). If in offering a sacrifice in the temple he remembers that a fellow believer has been offended by or is angry with him, he is to leave his gift at the altar, search out and be reconciled to his brother, and then return to offer the gift. But how many of Jesus' audience actually lived close enough to the temple in Jerusalem to fulfil this command literally? The Galileans who heard these words immediately realized that Jesus did not expect them, in such an event, to leave their gift at the altar (what if it were a lamb or goat?), go home to Galilee, seek reconciliation, return to Jerusalem in the hope that the gift would still be before the altar, and then offer it. Furthermore, a literal fulfilment of these words would be even more impossible for Jews from the Diaspora. The listeners therefore understood that the intent of Jesus' words did not lie in their literal meaning but rather in the general principle that one should not come into the presence of God without a willingness to seek reconciliation with one's brother.

On the other hand, the statement in Matthew 6:14-15 is to be taken literally. Whoever would seek the forgiveness of God must be willing to forgive others. Even as the experience of God's love causes the believer to love (1 John 4:19), so the contrition and repentance necessary for forgiveness cause us to forgive others who may be indebted to us (Matt.

18:23–35; Mark 11:26, LUKE 6:37). One cannot reach out with open hands to God for forgiveness and at the same time have a closed fist toward one's brother or neighbor. The words of Jesus in Matthew 6:14–15 are not an exaggeration. This teaching is literally true, and those who claim to take the teachings of Jesus seriously had best take these words at face value. Jesus intended that they be interpreted literally!

Within the Gospels are found numerous proverbial sayings of Jesus. In the next chapter we shall discuss various literary forms which are prone toward exaggeration, and we shall find that proverbs are clearly one of these forms. Because of the absolute manner in which they are usually stated, many proverbs which teach religious principles or truths are actually overstatements. Of the proverbs given below some require a rather literal interpretation and others demand that we recognize the presence of exaggeration.

Then Jesus said to him, "Put your sword back into its place; for all who take the sword will perish by the sword." [Matt. 26:52]

And Jesus said to them, "A prophet is not without honor, except in his own country, and among his own kin, and in his own house." [MARK 6:4]

And he said to them, "Take heed, and beware of all covetousness; for a man's life does not consist in the abundance of his possessions." [Luke 12:15]

You are the light of the world. A city set on a hill cannot be hid. [Matt. 5:14]

In comparing these four proverbs it appears that Luke 12:15 and Matthew 5:14 permit a rather straightforward, literal interpretation. Life does involve more than accumulation of possessions. Almost everyone would recognize that, to varying degrees, other factors are important: family, fame, power, influence, food, health. Very few in Jesus' audience would have claimed that all that matters in life is the possession of material goods. As for Matthew 5:14, it is simply a fact that cities built on the tops of hills cannot be hid. Jesus' audience would readily have acknowledged this. (Bear in mind that the people of that day were not acquainted with modern techniques of camouflage.)

On the other hand, it is also clear that while the proverb in Matthew 26:52 is generally true, not all who take the sword do indeed perish by it. On the contrary, some have found the sword quite profitable. Through service in war or as mercenaries, some people have obtained great wealth or power (perhaps even both). It is also the case that some great religious leaders during their lifetimes have been recognized and honored by their neighbors and relatives. This may indeed be rare, but it nevertheless does happen. The very fact that with regard to Matthew 26:52 and MARK 6:4 people can say, "Yes, that's true, but what about _____?" indicates that these proverbs are overstatements of general truths.

Although not closely related in theme, the two following examples show again the contrast between exaggerated and literal speech:

Again you have heard that it was said to the men of old, "You shall not swear falsely, but shall perform to the Lord what you have sworn." But I say to you, Do not swear at all, either by heaven, for it is the throne of God, or by the earth, for it is his footstool, or by Jerusalem, for it is the city of the great King. And do not swear by your head, for you cannot make one hair white or black. Let what you say be simply "Yes" or "No"; anything more than this comes from evil. [Matt. 5:33-37]

Whatever house you enter, first say, "Peace be to this house!" And if a son of peace is there, your peace shall rest upon him; but if not, it shall return to you. And remain in the same house, eating and drinking what they provide, for the laborer deserves his wages; do not go from house to house. . . . But whenever you enter a town and they do not receive you, go into its streets and say, "Even the dust of your town that clings to our feet, we wipe off against you." [LUKE 10:5-7, 10-11]

Even though there have been those who have interpreted

both of these passages quite literally, the early church fathers understood that these passages are not to be treated in the same manner. They recognized correctly that Matthew 5:33–37 is not to be understood as a literal prohibition against ever taking an oath. On the contrary, Augustine suggested, in light of the example of Paul in Romans 1:9 and Galatians 1:20, that Jesus was teaching that it is better not to swear and to tell the truth than to swear and to commit perjury. There is no sin in swearing to what is true, but due to our weak hearts we will best preserve ourselves from perjury by not swearing at all.[2] (For a number of additional indications that Jesus' teaching on oaths is an overstatement, see pp. 42–43, 45–46.)

On the other hand, the early church fathers interpreted quite literally Jesus' instructions on how itinerant preachers should conduct themselves in an unresponsive city. Hilary, for instance, explained that by wiping off the dust from their feet, missionaries would leave behind everything that belonged to the houses which they had entered.[3] Today, of course, the customs, dress, and general situation have changed considerably, so that a literal wiping off the dust from one's feet would be meaningless and impractical, but the audience of Luke (and Matthew—see the parallel account in MATT. 10:11–15) interpreted these words quite literally, even as Jesus' original hearers did.

There are times when even within a single pericope we find side by side examples of exaggeration and literal language. One such passage speaks of the danger that riches may cause to the individual:

Children, how hard it is to enter the kingdom of God! It is easier for a camel to go through the eye of a needle than for a rich man to enter the kingdom of God. [MARK 10:24b-25]

How hard it will be for those who have riches to enter the kingdom of God! [MARK 10:23]

There has been little difficulty in the past in interpreting verse 23 literally, since most scholars have agreed that riches do indeed pose a grave barrier to serving God. The biblical writer can even say that "the love of money is the root of all evils; it is through this craving that some have wandered away from the faith and pierced their hearts with many pangs" (1 Tim. 6:10). The hyperbolic nature of MARK 10:25, however, has resulted in a number of attempts to soften the force of this statement. Some have suggested that the Greek term *kamēlos* ("camel") should actually read *kamilos*, that is, "cable." The most common attempt to explain away the hyperbolic nature of this verse has been to claim that "the eye of a needle" refers to a small gate in the walls of Jerusalem through which a camel could barely pass. Such attempts are intended to rescue the saying from error, for whereas a camel cannot go through the eye of a (sewing) needle, some rich people do indeed enter the kingdom of God (see MATT. 27:57; MARK 15:42–46; Luke 8:1–3; 19:1–10 [esp. v. 2]). Such attempts to rescue this saying, however, are neither necessary nor helpful. There are several indications that the saying refers to a literal camel and a literal needle. First, the reaction of the disciples in MARK 10:26 indicates that they understood the saying as meaning that it is not merely difficult, but impossible for a rich person to enter the kingdom of God. Second, according to the textual evidence for Mark, and especially for Matthew and Luke, the best reading is "an eye of a needle," not "the eye of the needle." This indicates that we have here a general reference to sewing needles and camels rather than a specific reference to a particular gate in the walls of Jerusalem—"The Eye of the Needle." Finally, it should be noted that there exist several rabbinic sayings about an elephant's going through the eye of a needle.[4] What we have in our text, then, is a well-known idiom for great difficulty. Once we understand that Jesus' words are idiomatic and hyperbolic in nature, the attempts to explain them away become unnecessary.[5]

Finally, we will compare two of the ethical teachings of Jesus. At first glance it appears that Jesus is contradicting himself in his teachings here, but this, as we shall see later, is itself a clue that one of these sayings is an exaggeration.

If any one comes to me and does not hate his own father and mother and wife and children and brothers and sisters, yes, and even his own life, he cannot be my disciple. [LUKE 14:26]

And one of the scribes came up and heard them disputing with one another, and seeing that he answered them well, asked him, "Which commandment is the first of all?" Jesus answered, "The first is, 'Hear, O Israel: The Lord our God, the Lord is one; and you shall love the Lord your God with all your heart, and with all your soul, and with all your mind, and with all your strength.' The second is this, 'You shall love your neighbor as yourself.' There is no other commandment greater than these." And the scribe said to him, "You are right, Teacher; you have truly said that he is one, and there is no other but he; and to love him with all the heart, and with all the understanding, and with all the strength, and to love one's neighbor as oneself, is much more than all whole burnt offerings and sacrifices." And when Jesus saw that he answered wisely, he said to him, "You are not far from the kingdom of God." And after that no one dared to ask him any question. [MARK 12:28–34]

Although in our own day there are certain religious sects that have interpreted LUKE 14:26 quite literally and taught their converts to hate their parents, it is clear that this verse cannot be taken at face value. Exactly what Jesus meant by this saying may, at first glance, be somewhat unclear, but it is inconceivable that he intended for these words to be taken as meaning that his followers should literally hate their parents, wives, children, brothers, and sisters. Intuitively we know that this saying is not to be taken literally. Its very oddness constrains us to take a second look.[6] In the next chapter we shall discuss how and why the mind intuitively comes to this conclusion; for the present we need point out only that LUKE 14:26 is not a literal statement but an exaggerated one. On the other hand, the summary of the law given by Jesus in MARK 12:28–34 has universally been understood as being a literal and definitive statement of the essence of the Old Testament commandments. It was so understood not only by the apostles Paul (Rom. 13:8–10; Gal. 5:14) and James (2:8), but by the early church as well (Didache 1:2; 2:7; Barnabas 19:5; Gospel of Thomas 25).

The purpose of this chapter has been to call attention to the existence of exaggeration in the teachings of Jesus found in the canonical Gospels. Other examples could have been given, but after a certain point this becomes unnecessary, for our purpose in this chapter has not been to list all the examples of Jesus' use of exaggeration, but rather to demonstrate that such exaggeration truly exists.[7] While there may be debate as to the extent of exaggeration in the teachings of Jesus and as to the presence of exaggeration in a particular saying, the conclusion that Jesus did in fact use exaggeration in his teaching is inescapable.

Notes

1. For a helpful collection of the views of the early church fathers on this passage, see Thomas Aquinas, *Catena Aurea,* trans. John Henry Parker (Oxford: John Henry Parker, 1841), vol. 1, pp. 632–37.

2. Ibid., pp. 193–94.

3. Ibid., p. 378.

4. See b. (Babylonian Talmud) Baba Metzia 38b; b. Erubin 53a; b. Berachoth 55b.

5. G. B. Caird, *The Language and Imagery of the Bible* (Philadelphia: Westminster, 1980), p. 133, comments rather harshly on such attempts to explain this saying: "In this last instance plodding literalists have suggested that the needle's eye was the name for a low gate, like the door into the Church of the Nativity at Bethlehem, or that a camel was a kind of rope. But the Semitic bravura of Jesus' speech resists all such pathetic attempts to tame it." See also P. C. Sands, *Literary Genius of the New Testament* (Oxford: Clarendon, 1932), p. 77.

6. See Ian T. Ramsey, *Religious Language* (London: SCM, 1957), p. 95.

7. See Robert H. Stein, *The Method and Message of Jesus' Teachings* (Philadelphia: Westminster, 1978), pp. 8–12, for additional examples.

2

Recognizing Exaggeration in the Teachings of Jesus

There exist a number of helpful principles or canons by which one can detect if exaggeration is present in the teachings of Jesus. Most of these canons are also applicable in detecting the presence of exaggeration in other literature as well. Not all of them are, of course, equally valuable and not all are applicable in every instance. We shall also have to accept the fact that whereas it may be clear in certain instances that Jesus is using exaggeration, we may at other times not be certain whether Jesus is in fact using exaggeration or whether the magnitude of his actual demand only makes it look like exaggeration. We must be continually on our guard lest by carelessly labeling Jesus' calls to decision as examples of exaggeration, we water down their absolute nature. With this needed caution in view, we will find the following canons useful in detecting exaggeration in the sayings of Jesus.

CANON 1. **A statement which is literally impossible may contain exaggeration**

We have already divided Jesus' use of exaggeration into the two classifications of hyperbole and overstatement, and we have explained that whereas in overstatement the saying can be literally understood or literally carried out, in the case of hyperbole it cannot. Teachings can be impossible or hyperbolic in at least two ways: they can be physically impossible or they can be logically impossible. The particular teachings of Jesus which are physically impossible are simply inconceivable in light of our understanding of physical reality. Even in a world-view that accepts the supernatural, certain teachings of Jesus are clearly impossible; their impossibility was just as obvious to the original audience as it is to a present-day audience. In the case of logical impossibilities, we are dealing with intellectual or theological assertions that contradict logic or our basic understanding of God.

We can best demonstrate the difference between physical and logical impossibility by means of examples. Two examples of the former are:

> Why do you see the speck that is in your brother's eye, but do not notice the log that is in your own eye? Or how can you say to your brother, "Let me take the speck out of your eye," when there is the log in your own eye? You hypocrite, first take the log out of your own eye, and then you will see clearly to take the speck out of your brother's eye. [MATT. 7:3–5]

> Woe to you, scribes and Pharisees, hypocrites! for you tithe mint and dill and cummin, and have neglected the weightier matters of the law, justice and mercy and faith; these you ought to have done, without neglecting the others. You blind guides, straining out a gnat and swallowing a camel! [Matt. 23:23–24]

The impossibility of there being a log in a person's eye or of swallowing a camel is self-evident. Logs are simply too big to fit into a human eye and camels likewise too big to swallow. The hyperbole in these two passages serves to make Jesus' warnings against critically judging others and against religious hypocrisy most forceful and memorable.

Another example of a statement which is physically impossible to carry out is Matthew 6:2–4:

> Thus, when you give alms, sound no trumpet before you,

as the hypocrites do in the synagogues and in the streets, that they may be praised by men. Truly, I say to you, they have their reward. But when you give alms, do not let your left hand know what your right hand is doing, so that your alms may be in secret; and your Father who sees in secret will reward you.

How can one keep one's left hand from knowing what the right hand is doing? What can a hand know anyway? It is with the mind that a person knows. The hand has no means of knowing. Actually the saying is paradoxical in that Jesus tells us to make a conscious effort ("do not let") not to know what we are consciously doing (giving alms)!

One cannot help but think here of the similar use of hyperbolic language in the Old Testament. When God promised Abraham, "I will multiply your descendants as the stars of heaven and as the sand which is on the seashore" (Gen. 22:17), Abraham understood the exaggerated nature of the promise, for although he may not have known the total number of the stars in the heavens, he did have some idea of how much sand was on the seashore. Another example of a physical impossibility can be found in Isaiah 66:24, where the Lord says in judgment:

And they shall go forth and look on the dead bodies of the men that have rebelled against me; for their worm shall not die, their fire shall not be quenched, and they shall be an abhorrence to all flesh.

To have the worm present in a description of the judgment of the unrighteous is understandable; to have unquenchable fire present is likewise understandable; but to have both present together is not, for the fire would kill the worm. To claim that Isaiah conceived of a new kind of worm, an asbestos worm as it were, is to miss the point. The worm and the unquenchable fire are two well-known metaphorical portraits of judgment.[1] Placing them side by side simply reinforces Isaiah's proclamation of the certainty of the judgment. Additional Old Testament examples of physical impossibilities can be found in 2 Samuel 1:23; Job 38:7;

Psalm 19:1–4; Lamentations 2:11; and Amos 9:2–3.

Hyperbole can also be detected in instances of logical impossibility:

> All things are possible to him who believes. [Mark 9:23]

> Think not that I have come to abolish the law and the prophets; I have come not to abolish them but to fulfil them. For truly, I say to you, till heaven and earth pass away, not an iota, not a dot, will pass from the law until all is accomplished. [Matt. 5:17–18]

> You, therefore, must be perfect, as your heavenly Father is perfect. [MATT. 5:48]

The first example is clearly hyperbolic in that all things are simply not possible for the believer. He cannot become God! He cannot do away with the law of contradiction! He cannot cause God to cease existing! All things are therefore not logically possible for the believer. As for the second example, it is clear that it is logically impossible for iotas or dots to be fulfilled. Statements, promises, and hopes can be fulfilled, but letters (of the alphabet) and parts thereof cannot. And who can be as perfect as God? Who can be like the heavenly Father in any area of life? The hyperbole in this last example impresses upon us in a most powerful way the need to be gracious and merciful towards all even as God has been gracious and merciful towards us.[2]

CANON 2. A statement which conflicts with what Jesus says elsewhere may contain exaggeration

We assume that a reasonably intelligent person is logically consistent, and therefore we seek to interpret what he says in one place in the light of what he says elsewhere. It is a basic rule of hermeneutics that a particular teaching should be interpreted in the light of general teaching, that is, in light of its context.[3] Every teacher expects that his pupils will not take his words out of context. That context is the totality of what he has said or written elsewhere.[4] The term *harmonize* has fallen into disfavor due in part to past attempts to unify into a harmonious whole teachings that are clearly dissimilar. Nevertheless, any reasonably intelligent person hopes that whoever hears or reads his words will seek to harmonize his teachings, that is, to understand each teaching in the light of his other teachings.

Apart from any christological considerations, the least we can say of Jesus is that he was a reasonably intelligent person; we should therefore seek to understand his individual teachings in the light of the total context of his teachings. It may be that at times he does contradict in one place what he has said elsewhere, but courtesy requires that before we assume contradiction, we attempt to see if what appears to be contradictory may in fact not be contradictory at all. This courtesy should be extended to every speaker and writer unless there is sufficient evidence that the individual is in fact inconsistent.

As we look at various teachings of Jesus we do find statements that appear to conflict with one another; this conflict is often due to his use of exaggeration. Compare the following examples:

If any one comes to me and does not hate his own father and mother and wife and children and brothers and sisters, yes, and even his own life, he cannot be my disciple. [LUKE 14:26]

And he said to them, ''You have a fine way of rejecting the commandment of God, in order to keep your tradition! For Moses said, 'Honor your father and your mother'; and, 'He who speaks evil of father or mother, let him surely die'; but you say, 'If a man tells his father or his mother, What you would have gained from me is Corban' (that is, given to God)—then you no longer permit him to do anything for his father or mother, thus making void the word of God through your tradition which you hand on. And many such things you do." [MARK 7:9-13]

But when you pray, go into your room and shut the door and pray to your Father who is in secret; and your Father who sees in secret will reward you. [Matt. 6:6]

Pray then like this:
Our Father who art in
heaven,
Hallowed be thy name.
Thy kingdom done,
Thy will be done,
On earth as it is in
heaven.
Give us this day our daily
bread;
And forgive us our debts,
As we also have
forgiven our debtors;
And lead us not into
temptation,
But deliver us from evil.
[MATT. 6:9-13]

The scribes and the Pharisees sit on Moses' seat; so practice and observe whatever they tell you, but not what they do; for they preach, but do not practice. [Matt. 23:2-3]

Jesus said to them, "Take heed and beware of the leaven of the Pharisees and Sadducees. . . . How is it that you fail to perceive that I did not speak about bread? Beware of the leaven of the Pharisees and Sadducees." Then they understood that he did not tell them to beware of the leaven of bread, but of the teaching of the Pharisees and Sadducees. [MATT. 16:6; Matt. 16:11-12]

In isolation, LUKE 14:26 could be misunderstood as teaching hatred of one's family, but the minute one seeks to interpret this saying in the light of Jesus' teachings elsewhere (as in MARK 7:9–13; cf. also MARK 10:19), it becomes clear that we cannot take these words literally. Jesus is exaggerating for effect. He who taught his followers to love their enemies (LUKE 6:27) surely could not literally mean that they were to hate their own families. To do so would be to treat their families as enemies, which would in turn require the love for enemies which is commanded in LUKE 6:27! No, Jesus must be exaggerating in LUKE 14:26. (For a discussion of the idiomatic nature of "love-hate" language in the Bible see pp. 76–78.)

Jesus' command to pray only in one's closet (Matt. 6:6) conflicts with the corporate nature of the Lord's Prayer (MATT. 6:9–13), which, as we have already noted in the previous chapter, uses the first-person plural. Clearly the Evangelist who placed the Lord's Prayer immediately after the command to pray in secret did not think that Matthew 6:6 should be interpreted literally so as to contradict MATTHEW 6:9–13. No doubt he, like most Christians since, interpreted Jesus as teaching in 6:6 that personal prayer is not for show or for the applause of people but rather is a private matter between the believer and God.

With regard to the last example above, Jesus is in the one case condemning the Pharisees in certain particulars (MATT. 16:6; Matt. 16:11–12), and in the other case agreeing with them in general (Matt. 23:3). Only if we seek to find in both these passages an absolute reference to every single teaching of the Pharisees do we have an unresolvable problem. In general Jesus' teaching was similar to that of the Pharisees. The oral traditions which they observed he vigorously rejected (MARK 7:1–13), but doctrinally he was quite close to them in contrast to a group like the Sadducees (Acts 23:8). Could not a teacher or preacher today give similar advice concerning some well-known religious leaders? Rather than seeing in these two passages two contradictory statements of Jesus concerning the Pharisees, it is more reasonable to see in them two exaggerated, unqualified teachings concerning certain aspects of the Pharisees' doctrines and practices. The disciples were to be aware of the hypocritical nature of the Pharisees and the danger of the oral traditions; but inasmuch as the Pharisees sat on Moses' seat (i.e., in their role as teachers of the Old Testament), the disciples could for the most part practice what the Pharisees said the Old Testament taught. Surely this is a better way of understanding these two passages than to assume that Jesus was so dimwitted as to utter (and Matthew so dimwitted as to record) totally contradictory sayings about the Pharisees.[5]

We find a similar example of conflict within the Old Testament as well. In the Book of Isaiah two passages clearly conflict with each other. In describing the bliss of the coming period the prophet declares:

> The wolf shall dwell with the lamb, and the leopard shall lie down with the kid, and the calf and the lion and the fatling together, and a little child shall lead them. The cow and the bear shall feed; their young shall lie down together; and the lion shall eat straw like the ox. The sucking child shall play over the hole of the asp, and the weaned child shall put his hand on the adder's den. They shall not hurt or destroy in all my holy mountain; for the earth shall be full of the knowledge of the LORD as the waters cover the sea. [Isa. 11:6–9]

Yet later on we read a differing description:

> And a highway shall be there, and it shall be called the Holy Way; the unclean shall not pass over it, and fools shall not err therein. No lion shall be there, nor shall any ravenous beast come up on it; they shall not be found there, but the redeemed shall walk there. And the ransomed of the LORD shall return, and come to Zion with singing; everlasting joy shall be upon their heads; they shall obtain joy and gladness, and sorrow and sighing shall flee away. [Isa. 35:8–10]

Without entering into the issue of authorship, it is clear that Isaiah (or the last editor) placed these ostensibly contradictory passages within the text. Rather than attributing ineptitude to the author or editor, however, it is better to seek an interpretation which makes sense of the fact that both statements appear in the same work. Rather than understanding Isaiah 11:6-9 as teaching that in the coming period carnivorous animals will be transformed into herbivorous animals, it is better to see this passage as an exaggerated picture of the bliss and peace of the coming messianic age. Isaiah 35:8-10, with its statement that all nonpeaceful animals will be excluded, is, from a different angle, another idyllic picture of future bliss and peace. Both pictures, though literally contradictory, are in fact simply portraying via different analogies the very same reality—peace in the coming messianic age. The surface contradiction is an indication that at least one (perhaps both!) of the passages should not be interpreted literally but is an exaggerated description.

CANON 3. A statement which conflicts with the behavior and actions of Jesus elsewhere may contain exaggeration

Another signal that exaggeration may be present is a particular saying of Jesus which stands in sharp contrast to his behavior and actions. It is true that some religious teachers do not act in accordance with their teachings. Jesus knew this (Matt. 23:2-36, esp. vv. 2-3). Yet there are few people who would claim that Jesus did not practice what he preached. On the contrary, most scholars acknowledge that Jesus' life and actions are a perfect commentary on his teaching. If therefore a statement of Jesus conflicts with his behavior or actions elsewhere, we should consider the possibility that we have in this particular teaching an example of exaggeration. A clear instance of this is found in LUKE 14:26, which supposedly endorses hatred of one's parents and family. Surely this statement conflicts with the specific behavior of Jesus on the cross when he entrusted his mother into the care of the beloved disciple (John 19:26-27) as well as with the general nature of Jesus' entire ministry. It also conflicts with Luke's specific comment that Jesus "went down with [his parents] and came to Nazareth, and was obedient to them; and his mother kept all these things in her heart" (Luke 2:51).

A second example which we can note is MATTHEW 10:34, where Jesus states, "Do not think that I have come to bring peace on earth; I have not come to bring peace, but a sword." Not only do these words, if interpreted literally, conflict with what Jesus states elsewhere (cf. Matt. 5:9; 10:12–13; MARK 5:34; Luke 19:42), they conflict with his nonresistance when arrested at Gethsemane (MARK 14:43–50) and his forgiveness of his enemies from the cross (Luke 23:34). The context in which MATTHEW 10:34 is found also indicates that the Evangelist understood that the sword Jesus had in view had nothing to do with politics or military activity, but was a metaphorical description of the division that faith in Christ can and sometimes does bring within the family unit when one member becomes a follower of Jesus and the others do not (MATT. 10:35–39).

Another example that can be mentioned in this regard is the conflict between Jesus' own practice of prayer and his teaching on the subject. In Matthew 6:6 Jesus states that prayer should be offered in one's own room with the door shut; nevertheless, even though Jesus himself did at times seek privacy in order to pray, he did not always pray in his closet (MARK 6:46; 14:32; Luke 6:12; LUKE 9:28). At times, furthermore, Jesus prayed publicly as well (MATT. 19:13— Mark and Luke in the parallel accounts simply mention Jesus' touching of the children, but he no doubt also prayed a blessing upon them as Matthew states; cf. Gen. 48:17–20).

A final example that can be mentioned is Jesus' teaching on swearing in Matthew 5:33–37:

> Again you have heard that it was said to the men of old, "You shall not swear falsely, but shall perform to the Lord what you have sworn." But I say to you, Do not swear at all, either by heaven, for it is the throne of God, or by the earth, for it is his footstool, or by Jerusalem, for it is the city of the great King. And do not swear by your head, for you cannot make one hair white or black. Let what you say be simply "Yes" or "No"; anything more than this comes from evil.

At first glance this passage might be interpreted as an absolute prohibition against swearing in any form. Jesus' teaching in Matthew 23:16–22 should, however, make us cautious of such an interpretation. In this passage Jesus condemns the view of the Pharisees that swearing by the temple or the altar amounts to nothing (since no one could hold a lien on the temple or the altar against the one who made the oath), whereas swearing by the gold of the temple or the gift that one is to offer on the altar makes the oath binding (in that a lien could be placed on them). Here Jesus is not totally prohibiting swearing but is rebuking the way in which certain Pharisees made oaths. What is decisive, however, with regard to Matthew 5:33–37 is the fact that Jesus himself was willing to be placed under oath. We read that Jesus was silent at his trial (MATT. 26:63a); but when the high priest said, "I adjure you by the living God, tell us if you are the Christ, the Son of God" (Matt. 26:63b), Jesus no longer remained silent but responded. According to the law (Lev. 5:1; see also 1 Kings 22:16 and Prov. 29:24), when placed under an oath ("a public adjuration") one could not remain silent. There was no pleading of the fifth amendment here! To remain silent was to admit one's guilt. Jesus by his response to the high priest revealed that he accepted the validity of oaths. It seems clear by his action here that Jesus did not interpret his teaching in Matthew 5:33–37 as prohibiting his swearing under oath in this instance.

CANON 4. A statement which conflicts with the teachings of the Old Testament may contain exaggeration

Another factor that should alert the reader to the possible presence of exaggeration is conflict between a particular teaching of Jesus and the teachings of the Old Testament. Much has been written concerning Jesus' view of the Old Testament and of the law, and widely opposing positions have been advanced. Some see the New Testament faith as standing in opposition to the Old Testament religion. Frequently the Matthean antitheses ("You have heard that it was said . . ."—Matt. 5:21, 27, 33, 38, 43) are offered as support for this view. The New Testament faith is furthermore often portrayed as pure gospel and grace whereas the Old Testament is supposedly sheer law and works, and we of course ''are not under law but under grace'' (Rom. 6:14). This view, which misunderstands Paul at this point, was held by Marcion and various Gnostic groups early in the history of the church, but was rightly seen to be heretical. Others see in both Old and New Testament a single covenant of grace with very little difference between them. This was the view held by many of the early church fathers in opposition to Marcion. The truth, however, lies in neither of these two extremes, for the new covenant (i.e., the New Testament) is not a religion which originated in A.D. 30 but the same faith held by Abraham, Isaac, and Jacob (Gal. 3:6–9), and yet it is a *new* covenant as well (Heb. 8). We should therefore not be surprised to see elements of both continuity and newness in Jesus' teaching.

What, then, was Jesus' view toward the Old Testament? Jesus did not see himself as usurping the law and the prophets, but rather as fulfilling them (Matt. 5:17–19).[6] In the Old Testament commandments, *correctly understood,* there was life (MARK 10:17–19), and Jesus' own summary of his ethical teachings consisted of two Old Testament commands (Deut. 6:5 and Lev. 19:18) which in turn summarized all the Old Testament commandments (MARK 12:28–34). His strong antagonism towards the oral traditions of the Pharisees was due to the fact that these traditions countered the Old Testament commandments (MARK 7:8–13). At a few points Jesus did suggest that the Old Testament commandments were outdated because of the coming of the kingdom of God (Matt. 5:38–39; MARK 7:14–23; 10:2–12), but these instances are few in number. It would appear, then, that unless Jesus taught explicitly to the contrary, he regarded the ethical teachings of the Old Testament to be the revealed will of God and still binding. So if we find a teaching of Jesus which conflicts with the Old Testament, it is quite possibly an example of exaggeration.

Once again we raise the example of LUKE 14:26. In light of the commandment to honor one's father and mother

(Exod. 20:12; Deut. 5:16) and in light of the frequent Old Testament emphasis in this area (Lev. 19:3; Prov. 10:1; 15:20; 23:22), it would be strange indeed to think that Jesus was actually commanding his followers to hate their parents.

Another example can be found in Matthew 5:33–37. The apparent prohibition of swearing raises the issue of what to do with all the Old Testament references in which swearing is seen as perfectly acceptable (Lev. 5:1; 19:12 [cf. Exod. 20:7]; Num. 30:2–15; Deut. 23:21–23). To these can be added the many instances in the Old Testament in which God himself is described as having sworn (Deut. 1:8; Ps. 110:4; 132:11; Isa. 14:24; Ezek. 20:5). These many references make it doubtful whether Jesus was actually forbidding in Matthew 5:33–37 all instances of swearing, for knowing full well of the many times when God had sworn an oath, Jesus would certainly never have issued a command which might seem to imply that God himself was wrong in so doing.

CANON 5. A statement which conflicts with other teachings in the New Testament may contain exaggeration

Conflict between a particular teaching of Jesus and other New Testament passages may also be a clue to the presence of exaggeration in Jesus' words. We must be aware, however, that this canon does not serve as an infallible guide. It is certainly possible that the writers of the New Testament misunderstood various teachings of Jesus. Indeed, there have been many extravagant claims to the effect that they did in fact greatly misunderstand his words and that we are now just beginning to understand what he truly meant. C. S. Lewis has warned, however, against scholarly presumption of this nature: "The idea that any man or writer should be opaque to those who lived in the same culture, spoke the same language, shared the same habitual imagery and unconscious assumptions, and yet be transparent to those who have none of these advantages, is in my opinion preposterous."[7] Without denying the possibility of misunderstanding on the part of the New Testament writers, it nevertheless appears reasonable to assume that if they did not interpret a particular teaching of Jesus literally, apparently regarding it instead as exaggerative in nature, they were probably correct in so doing.

A good example is Jesus' teaching on swearing in Matthew 5:33–37. In both Acts 2:30 and Hebrews 6:16–17; 7:20–22 we read of God's swearing in order to emphasize the absolute certainty of his promises. Moreover, we know that Paul did not believe that Jesus taught an absolute prohibition of swearing, for the apostle voluntarily "call[s] God to witness" (2 Cor. 1:23), declares that "before God, I do not lie" (Gal. 1:20), and proclaims that "God is my witness" (Rom. 1:9; Phil. 1:8). It is true that James 5:12 reiterates Jesus' prohibition in Matthew 5:33–37, but it would seem best to conclude that James, like Jesus, was by the use of exaggeration emphasizing the danger of a routine swearing of oaths in daily speech, a practice which was prevalent in his day. One's character should be such that a simple yes or no will suffice.

Another example is found in the same chapter of the Sermon on the Mount. In MATTHEW 5:42 Jesus states, "Give to him who begs from you, and do not refuse him who would borrow from you." Yet within the New Testament there is at least one clear example in which the church is told not to grant the requests of those who beg. In seeking to remedy the problem of those at Thessalonica who, because of their belief in the nearness of the parousia, were no longer working but living off their Christian friends, the apostle Paul states, "For even when we were with you, we gave you this command: If any one will not work, let him not eat" (2 Thess. 3:10). Rather than seeing a contradiction between Jesus and the apostle, it is more reasonable to conclude that Jesus, in teaching of the need to be generous, was exaggerating in MATTHEW 5:42 simply because he did not want to list various exceptions to the general rule. To have listed exceptions would have changed the meaning, for the focus would then have shifted to the exceptions. Surely it is not unreasonable to think that Jesus would have agreed with Paul's injunction not to give to those who were begging if giving to them what they asked would perpetuate their deficiencies (laziness).

Another saying of Jesus which other passages in the New Testament do not interpret literally is MATTHEW 7:1: "Judge not, that you be not judged." Similar teaching is found in Romans 14:10 and 1 Corinthians 4:5. Yet how can one obey MATTHEW 7:1 literally and practice the kind of discipline taught in the rest of the New Testament? How can one rebuke (1 Tim. 5:20; 2 Tim. 4:2) or pronounce judgment (1 Cor. 5:3)? Paul even rebukes the Corinthian Christians because they failed to judge when they should have (1 Cor. 6:1–6). August Tholuck's advice concerning such sayings of Jesus can still be quoted with profit: "we must never forget that they are to be interpreted according to the analogia fidei, according to the whole scope of the Christian doctrine, according to the spirit of Christ."[8]

CANON 6. A statement which is interpreted by another Evangelist in a nonliteral way may contain exaggeration

Anyone who has ever used a harmony of the Gospels has noticed that the sayings of Jesus occasionally occur in slightly different forms in the different Gospels. Frequently such differences are due to grammatical considerations, but there are times when the differences have theological significance. In seeking to determine if a particular saying of Jesus is an example of exaggeration, we can at times be assisted by comparing the saying under investigation with its parallel in another Gospel. If the parallel qualifies the suspected exaggeration, it is reasonable to assume that this Evangelist sought to clarify Jesus' original saying (his *ipsissima verba*) by expressing the meaning of Jesus' exaggerated statement in a form less likely to be misunderstood. It may, of course, be the case that the exaggeration is due to the Evangelist's attempt to heighten Jesus' original teaching, but usually we find that the exaggeration was part of the original.

A good example is found in LUKE 14:26 and its parallel in MATTHEW 10:37:

If any one comes to me and does not hate his own father and mother and wife and children and brothers and sisters, yes, and even his own life, he cannot be my disciple. [LUKE 14:26]	He who loves father or mother more than me is not worthy of me; and he who loves son or daughter more than me is not worthy of me. [MATT. 10:37]

It is reasonably certain that in this particular instance Luke's account is closer to the actual words of Jesus. Matthew, however, is nevertheless true to the teaching of Jesus at this point; although Matthew uses a different wording, he does not change the meaning or sense of Jesus' saying. Through the form of the saying in Matthew, we are able to see that Jesus' original command to hate one's family was not meant to be taken literally but was an exaggeration used for effect. "Hate" is simply an idiomatic way of saying "love less." In this instance the exaggerated nature of LUKE 14:26 is evident not only from the fact that it conflicts with what Jesus says elsewhere (canon 2), with Jesus' behavior (canon 3), with the teachings of the Old Testament (canon 4), and with other passages in the New Testament (canon 5), but also from the fact that the Evangelist Matthew obviously understood Jesus' actual words as an overstatement.

A second example is the "exception clause" in Jesus' teaching on divorce. We find the teaching in its absolute form in three instances and with the exception clause in two:

And he said to them, "Whoever divorces his wife and marries another, commits adultery against her." [MARK 10:11]	And I say to you: whoever divorces his wife, except for unchastity, and marries another, commits adultery. [MATT. 19:9]
Every one who divorces his wife and marries another commits adultery, and he who marries a woman divorced from her husband commits adultery. [LUKE 16:18]	But I say to you that every one who divorces his wife, except on the ground of unchastity, makes her an adulteress; and whoever marries a divorced woman commits adultery. [MATT. 5:32]

To the married I give charge,
not I but the Lord, that the
wife should not separate
from her husband (but if she
does, let her remain single or
else be reconciled to her husband)—and that the hus-
band should not divorce his
wife. [1 Cor. 7:10–11]

Although some would argue the reverse, most scholars believe that the unqualified form of the saying in Mark, Luke, and 1 Corinthians is closer to Jesus' actual words than are the Matthean versions with the exception clause. In the three non-Matthean versions we have a more authentic teaching of Jesus on divorce.[9] Some have suggested that Matthew by including the exception clause has in fact rejected the absoluteness of Jesus' teaching on this matter. According to this view, Matthew realized that the teaching of Jesus would be quite unpalatable to his Jewish-Christian audience and therefore perverted it. But is such a harsh judgment upon the writer of the first Gospel necessary or even warranted?

We have already established that Jesus made frequent use of exaggeration. Is it possible that his saying on divorce is an exaggeration, and that Matthew introduces the exception clause to bring out its true meaning? Let us for a moment suggest the following scenario as a possible context for Jesus' teaching on the subject. Jesus walks into the midst of a rabbinic debate on divorce. The debate among the Pharisees on this issue is a lively one, and the views range from the conservative position of Shammai, who argues via a narrow interpretation of Deuteronomy 24:1 that the only cause for divorce is unchastity, to that of the liberal Hillel, who interprets Deuteronomy 24:1 broadly and concludes that a burned supper or even finding a more attractive woman is a just cause for divorce. Jesus, being asked his view on divorce (MARK 10:2), realizes that the whole debate is focusing upon speculations about when the divine plan for marriage can be ignored. Out of concern for the

basic plan and purpose of God in marriage he replies
abruptly, "There is no good reason for breaking the divine
rule!" In so doing Jesus is not so much concerned with
hypothetical speculations on exceptions as he is zealous for
the perfect purpose of God, which does not involve divorce.
That Jesus is not seeking to lay down here a legal dictum
to cover every situation is understood both by Paul and by
Matthew, for Paul does grant an exception (1 Cor. 7:15) as
does Matthew. One might, as has been mentioned, see Paul
and Matthew as corruptors of Jesus' teaching in this area;
but if we believe that Jesus is employing overstatement in
this instance, we will instead see the canonical writers as
authoritative interpreters who bring out the sense of what
Jesus actually means by his teaching.[10]

Another example in which an Evangelist by his redac-
tion clearly indicates that he understands Jesus' teaching
to be exaggerated involves the controversial saying of Jesus
found in MATTHEW 10:34:

Do not think that I have come to bring peace on earth; I have not come to bring peace, but a sword. [MATT. 10:34]	Do you think that I have come to give peace on earth? No, I tell you, but rather division. [LUKE 12:51]

It is almost certain that the Matthean version of this saying
is authentic, for it is far easier to understand why one would
change "sword" to "division" than to understand why one
would change "division" to "sword." The desire of the
church to disassociate itself from anything that could be
misconstrued as teaching political revolution or rebellion
would have as a consequence a strong inclination to change
"sword" to "division" and an even stronger reluctance to
change "division" to "sword." That Jesus himself was not
a political revolutionary, that is, a Zealot, and had no sym-
pathies in that direction is evident from such passages as
MATTHEW 5:38–42 (esp. v. 39); Matthew 26:52; MARK
12:13–17; and LUKE 6:27–29. Furthermore, it is evident from
the context, as we shall immediately see, that Jesus was not

concerned here with political revolt or rebellion but rather with family divisions. Luke, understanding the exaggerated nature of Jesus' saying and the possibility of its being misunderstood, therefore used "division" to describe the dissension and disruption that Jesus brings to homes in which some believe in him and others do not.

In addition to modifying the wording, another way in which an Evangelist can reveal that he does not interpret a saying of Jesus literally is by means of the context into which he places the saying. An example is the statement just discussed, where Jesus asserts that he did not come to bring peace on earth but a sword (MATT. 10:34). The context that follows clearly indicates that Matthew does not interpret this saying politically or militarily at all, for in what follows we read of family strife (v. 35) and the need to love Jesus more than family (v. 37)! From this it is clear that Matthew interprets the saying he records in 10:34 as a metaphor about the family strife and discord that sometimes result from following Jesus Christ.

In a similar manner the apparently absolute and unconditional "Judge not, that you be not judged" (Matt. 7:1), is followed in the next verse by the warning that God will judge us by the same standard by which we judge others (and for Matthew, God's judgment of the world is inevitable).[11] There follow the warning against seeing a speck in our brother's eye and not seeing the log in our own (vv. 3–5), and the command not to give to dogs what is holy or to throw our pearls before swine (v. 6). This command of course entails making a judgment regarding to whom we are not to give what is holy. Matthew clearly did not see any conflict between the prohibition of judging in verse 1 and the judging described and commanded in the following verses. In addition to these references it must be noted that Matthew 18:15–17 (cf. also LUKE 17:3) prescribes how the church should proceed in matters of church discipline. Obviously the prohibition in Matthew 7:1 does not exclude the church discipline prescribed in Matthew 18:15–17. This is possible only if Matthew 7:1 is understood as an example of overstatement.

CANON 7. A statement which the audience of Jesus did not interpret literally may contain exaggeration

If we assume that Jesus not only sought to communicate certain truths and realities to his listeners, but that he effectively did so, we must also assume that his audience understood, for the most part at least, his teachings. This does not deny the fact that frequently his audience misunderstood his teachings, and that their failure in this regard may even at times have been Jesus' intent (MARK 4:10–12; 7:17–18). Nevertheless the primary purpose of any prophet, teacher, or evangelist is to convey his message to his audience in a way that will enable them to understand what he is trying to say. No one teaches with a goal of being totally incomprehensible! Do we find in the Gospels any occasions when Jesus' audience interpreted a saying of his as being an exaggeration? If so, this may provide a guide for us. But how can we know how Jesus' audience interpreted his teachings? Even if we grant that the Gospels of Matthew and John were written by eyewitnesses, or if we grant that all of the teachings of Jesus recorded in the Gospels came ultimately from eyewitnesses (Luke 1:1–4) who were aware how the audience interpreted his teachings, the fact remains that the Gospel writers were not primarily concerned with recording how his audience interpreted his words. Furthermore, the very arrangement of Jesus' teachings into collections or blocks such as the Sermon on the Mount compounds the problem, for it is impossible in such instances to know how the audience of Jesus reacted to a particular saying in that collection. It must be confessed with all candor, then, that the applicability of this canon is extremely limited.

There are, however, some instances in which the response of Jesus' audience is recorded and provides a clue for us. It is evident from MARK 10:22 that the rich young ruler understood that, for him at least, the command of Jesus to ''go, sell what you have, and give to the poor'' (MARK 10:21) was not an overstatement, but was meant to be taken quite literally, for we read that the young man's countenance fell and he went away sorrowful. On the other hand, the opposition of the Pharisees toward Jesus and his followers would tend to indicate that Matthew 23:2 was not interpreted in a completely literal way by Jesus' audience. Another passage where this canon might be applicable is the conversation of Jesus with the Syrophoenician woman in MARK 7:24–30. To the woman's request that he heal her daughter he replied, ''Let the children first be fed, for it is not right to take the children's bread and throw it to the dogs'' (MARK 7:27). It is clear that the woman did not understand Jesus' metaphorical language as a literal refusal. On the contrary she understood it as the beginning of a dialogue. She understood his meaning to be: ''The children should be fed first, shouldn't they? It is not right to take the children's bread and throw it to the dogs, is it?'' In view of the fact that she continued the dialogue and responded both in faith and with wit, ''Yes, Lord; yet even the dogs under the table eat the children's crumbs'' (v. 28), Jesus granted her request and healed her daughter.

CANON 8. A statement which has not been literally fulfilled may contain exaggeration

There are times when the exaggerated nature of a saying of Jesus suggests itself by the fact that the statement has not been literally fulfilled in history or practice. The exaggerated nature of MARK 13:2—''Do you see these great buildings? There will not be left here one stone upon another, that will not be thrown down''—is evident from history itself. Some of those stones still stand one upon the other! The prophecy's meaning was nevertheless clearly fulfilled in the destruction that befell Jerusalem in A.D. 70. The actual intent of the statement, but not the affective expression used to convey it, has been carried out.

Other examples of non-fulfilment are various sayings on prayer:

> Ask, and it will be given you; seek, and you will find; knock, and it will be opened to you. For every one who asks

> receives, and he who seeks finds, and to him who knocks it will be opened. [MATT. 7:7-8]

> And Jesus answered them, "Have faith in God. Truly, I say to you, whoever says to this mountain, 'Be taken up and cast into the sea,' and does not doubt in his heart, but believes that what he says will come to pass, it will be done for him. Therefore I tell you, whatever you ask in prayer, believe that you receive it, and you will." [MARK 11:22-24]

To these references can be added Matthew 18:19; Luke 11:5-8; LUKE 11:9-13; and John 14:13; 15:7, 16; 16:23-24. Although some of these promises are qualified (MARK 11:22-24 requires faith—one must not doubt but believe; Matt. 18:19 requires two people agreeing in prayer; John 15:7 requires abiding in Christ; John 14:13; 15:16; and 16:23-24 require asking in Jesus' name), MATTHEW 7:7-8 and the parallel in LUKE 11:5-13 have no qualification at all. The problem which a literal interpretation of these verses creates is self-evident. Christians through the centuries have at times asked and not received, sought and not found, knocked and not been opened unto. Furthermore, at times they have, abiding in Christ and asking in his name, prayed in large numbers (far more than two or three) and with great faith, doubting nothing. But to no apparent avail!

How are we to explain this? One could, of course, say that frequently Christians have prayed wrongly and that God in his mercy and wisdom has not granted their requests. James 4:3 ("You ask and do not receive, because you ask wrongly, to spend it on your passions") can be mentioned in this regard.[12] No doubt Jesus would have agreed wholeheartedly with the teaching of this verse. He in fact expected his listeners to assume certain qualifications. He expected them to assume that they should not ask for anything that would dishonor God or impair their physical-moral-mental-emotional-spiritual growth as children of God. Note, however, that the emphasis of Jesus' teaching concerning prayer is God's loving and gracious desire to bless his children, not a list specifying things that we ought not to pray for. As a result he did not incorporate any qualifications in his teaching on prayer, even though he expected that his hearers would assume them. This omission of qualifications in these sayings of Jesus on prayer signifies that we are dealing here with exaggeration. It is interesting to note that when the Evangelists recorded these examples of Jesus' use of overstatement, they likewise expected their readers to be able to recognize them as such.[13]

Our final example of the principle that a lack of fulfilment of certain sayings of Jesus may be a signal that we are dealing with an exaggerated form of teaching on the part of Jesus is Matthew 26:52 (not all warriors die young!).

CANON 9. A statement which, if literally fulfilled, would not achieve the desired goal may contain exaggeration

We have still another clue to the possible presence of exaggeration if the literal fulfilment of a particular saying would not achieve what Jesus intended.[14] This canon applies primarily to various exhortations given by Jesus. If we were to take the words of Jesus in MATTHEW 5:29–30 literally and mutilate our bodies, would we achieve the goal Jesus sought? Would the removal of the right eye keep one from lusting (note the context of Matt. 5:28)? Would the removal of both eyes accomplish this? From where does lust arise? Can one not lust in the dark with both eyes shut? And are hands the cause of sin? Are they not, rather, simply instruments by which the sinful heart carries out its lusts? To interpret these words literally is to assume that Jesus naively believed that the mutilation of one's eyes or hands could protect us from sin, but this is clearly contradicted by Jesus' teaching elsewhere (canon 2) that it is what comes out of a person, that is, out of his heart, that defiles him (MARK 7:20–23). What Jesus is seeking in MATTHEW 5:29–30 is for us to remove from our lives anything that would keep us from entering the kingdom of God. He is seeking repentance. Repentance does not involve mutilation of our bodily members, which are God-given gifts and vehicles by which he may be served, but mutilation of our fallen Adamic nature. This involves the inner man, not our external members. Literal fulfilment of MATTHEW 5:29–30 would therefore not bring about the desired goal. On the contrary, it could actually cause us to lose sight of the real problem by focusing on the symptoms instead.

Another example is found in Matthew 6:3–4. Keeping one's left hand from knowing what the right hand is doing would not necessarily bring about Jesus' goal of secrecy in our giving. Others still might know. To use a ridiculous illustration: one could perhaps sound a trumpet each time one intends for the left hand to cease paying attention to what the right is doing. With careful conditioning the sound of the trumpet could immediately cause the left hand not to know what the right hand is doing and at the same time signal to all those in the vicinity that they should note our generous giving! Of course, all of this is impossible, but it does demonstrate that a literal carrying out of what Jesus commands in these verses would not bring about what Jesus is seeking. As a result it is reasonable to conclude that we have here a case of exaggeration for effect.

CANON 10. Statements which make use of particular literary forms are prone to exaggeration

In the introduction we mentioned that certain literary forms are more prone to exaggeration than are others. Whereas doctors' reports, laboratory analyses, chemistry textbooks, and automobile manuals must be literal, we tend to expect exaggeration in love letters, fish stories, and descriptions of grandchildren. Likewise in both the Old and New Testaments there are certain literary forms which tend to use exaggerated language. They include proverbs, prophecy, poetry, metaphor, and parables.

Exaggeration in proverbs

A proverb is a brief, pithy saying which is known through nature or experience and presents some general truth in a striking manner. These truths are usually available for all to see; thus, wisdom literature is not limited to the Bible. The wisdom literature of the Bible has, in fact, many parallels in nonbiblical literature. The main difference between biblical and nonbiblical proverbs does not lie in their form or even in their content, but rather in the fact that biblical proverbs are presented not only in the light of nature and experience that is available to all, but also in the context of the revelation of God found in the Old and New Testaments.

Proverbs by their very nature are prone to exaggeration because they tend to express a general truth in compressed form and in universal language. They also tend to use sharp contrasts and paradox. "Most proverbs are remembered chiefly, not because of the truth they reveal, but because they are in the form of a general or universal hyperbolic statement not encumbered by exceptions and limitations."[15] Perhaps the best way of demonstrating this character of proverbs is simply to quote a number of them. First we shall present a number of Old Testament proverbs which use universal language to express a general truth and reality:

> Honor the LORD with your substance and with the first fruits of all your produce; then your barns will be filled with plenty, and your vats will be bursting with wine. [Prov. 3:9-10]

> The LORD does not let the righteous go hungry, but he thwarts the craving of the wicked. A slack hand causes poverty, but the hand of the diligent makes rich. [Prov. 10:3-4]

> Misfortune pursues sinners, but prosperity rewards the righteous. [Prov. 13:21]

> A soft answer turns away wrath, but a harsh word stirs up anger. [Prov. 15:1]

> A slave who deals wisely will rule over a son who acts shamefully, and will share the inheritance as one of the brothers. [Prov. 17:2]

> Train up a child in the way he should go, and when he is old he will not depart from it. [Prov. 22:6]

> He who oppresses the poor to increase his own wealth, or gives to the rich, will only come to want. [Prov. 22:16]

The wisdom and truthfulness of these proverbs would be accepted by almost all. Hard work does, more often than not, bring prosperity. A soft answer frequently does avoid confrontation and hostility. Even Proverbs 17:2, although not a usual occurrence in life, nevertheless serves as a truthful warning to sons that they should not act shamefully lest they lose their inheritance. (For a servant or slave to share in the inheritance of his master was not impossible in biblical times, although it would have been unheard of in America in the first part of the nineteenth century.) It is also true that individuals taught to love and serve the Lord in their childhood will remain faithful to their God and continue to serve him during their years as adults. Yet this is not always true. There are exceptions. Godly parents who have sought to raise their children in the fear and admonition of the Lord have seen them become reprobate and apostate. Both Eli and Samuel had that experience (1 Sam. 2:12; 8:5). Of course, one could say that Eli and Samuel (and all parents today whose children do not walk in the ways of the Lord) did not train their children perfectly. But which parents whose children have become true followers and servants of God can boast that they trained their children perfectly? Proverbs 22:6 is a general truth expressed in universal language: the normal experience is that children raised to love the Lord will serve him ás adults. This is not, however, a law of life which holds 100 percent of the time. It is also obvious that there are hard-working people who do not prosper and tithers who do not possess great wealth. A proverb by its very nature often evokes the response, ''Yes, but...,'' that is to say, ''Yes, I agree in principle that this is true, but there are exceptions.''[16] This response does not nullify the value of the proverb. We must understand that the genre seeks to present in universal language a general truth concerning life in the light of the revelation of God in nature and in his written Word.

With this in mind let us look at some of the proverbs of Jesus:

Where your treasure is, there will your heart be also. [MATT. 6:21]

A disciple is not above his teacher, nor a servant above his master. [MATT. 10:24]

Out of the abundance of the heart the mouth speaks. [MATT. 12:34b]

All who take the sword will perish by the sword. [Matt. 26:52c]

A prophet is not without honor, except in his own country, and among his own kin, and in his own house. [MARK 6:4]

He who is faithful in a very little is faithful also in much; and he who is dishonest in a very little is dishonest also in much. [Luke 16:10]

That these proverbs of Jesus are general truths which are simply confirmed by the exceptions is evident. Most people who are faithful in small matters are indeed faithful in large ones as well. Yet there are people who do not steal the pennies of others but, when a really big opportunity comes, find the temptation irresistible. Some people also speak not out of their hearts but with forked tongue. The same mouth can pronounce blessings and cursings (James 3:10). Although James gives three proverbs in question form which suggest that this is impossible (3:11–12), he nevertheless knows that believers do use their tongues to bring curses as well as blessings. This, he declares, ought not to be (3:10b).

From these examples it is clear that the proverbial form is prone to exaggeration. By its very nature it is so inclined. This is not always true, however, for there are proverbs that are universal and without exception (MATT. 6:27; 10:26; Luke 12:15; 14:11). Nevertheless, we should be aware that many proverbs do use exaggeration, and they should be interpreted accordingly.

Exaggeration in prophecy

Another form inclined toward the use of exaggeration is prophecy.[17] This does not mean that all of the details of prophetic literature are exaggerated. Rather, it means that some prophecy is not so much concerned with an exact literal description of future events as with a picturesque portrayal of those events. Some prophetic literature is not so much a photographic picture of what is to occur as an impressionistic painting. Furthermore, we must also understand that a future prophecy of judgment which appears absolute and irreversible always assumes that if the people repent, the judgment that is prophesied will be stayed. Messages of judgment are proclaimed in the hope that upon hearing them, the people will repent and avoid the judgment foretold. All of these warnings carry with them an unexpressed "unless they repent." In fact many times events are foretold precisely in order that they not come to pass.[18]

An example is Jonah 3:4: "Yet forty days, and Nineveh shall be overthrown!" We read shortly thereafter that "when God saw what [the Ninevites] did, how they turned from their evil way, God repented of the evil which he had said he would do to them; and he did not do it" (3:10). That Jonah knew that his proclamation entailed this very possibility is clear from 4:1–2: "But it displeased Jonah exceedingly, and he was angry. And he prayed to the LORD and said, 'I pray thee, LORD, is not this what I said when I was yet in my country? That is why I made haste to flee to Tarshish; for I knew that thou art a gracious God and merciful, slow to anger, and abounding in steadfast love, and repentest of evil.' " Jonah knew from the beginning that his prophecy was not simply a prediction of future events. If it had been simply a prediction, he would have relished his task. His prophecy, however, was not simply a prediction but rather a warning to Nineveh. This is why he sought to flee from God. He did not want to preach to the people of Nineveh because he knew that they might repent and thus stave off the divine judgment. And Jonah wanted Nineveh damned!

Another example of a prophecy which was capable of being halted even though it appeared in absolute form is found in Isaiah 38:1. Isaiah says to Hezekiah, "Thus says the LORD: Set your house in order; for you shall die, you shall not recover." Yet in the following verses we read that God granted to Hezekiah his request and gave to him fifteen more years of life. Still another example is found in Micah 3:12, where Micah prophesies of the destruction of Jerusalem. We know from Jeremiah 26:16-19 that this prophecy was averted due to the repentance of the people.

These examples demonstrate that all prophecies of judgment must be interpreted in light of the principle found in Jeremiah 18:7-8: "If at any time I declare concerning a nation or kingdom, that I will pluck up and break down and destroy it, and if that nation, concerning which I have spoken, turns from its evil, I will repent of the evil that I intended to do to it" (see also 1 Kings 21:20-29). From this passage and the examples given, it is clear that prophecies of judgment which are stated in absolute form can be reversed if repentance is forthcoming. Similarly, prophecies of blessing can be reversed in case of apostasy (Jer. 18:9-10). By their very nature, then, all such prophecies are exaggerated.

The impressionistic quality of much prophetic literature is another cause of exaggeration. Note the following example:

> Behold, the day of the LORD comes, cruel, with wrath and fierce anger, to make the earth a desolation and to destroy its sinners from it. For the stars of the heavens and their constellations will not give their light; the sun will be dark at its rising and the moon will not shed its light. I will punish the world for its evil, and the wicked for their iniquity; I

will put an end to the pride of the arrogant, and lay low
the haughtiness of the ruthless. [Isa. 13:9–11]

The prophecy given here is addressed to Babylon (13:1, 19).
God will judge Babylon for her many evils. This is certain!
Yet the terminology used is certainly not literal, for the stars
and moon did not cease giving their light and the sun was
not dark in its rising when Babylon fell to the Persians in
539 B.C. We have here, in the idiomatic language of judgment, picturesque descriptions of the impending destruction of the Babylonian Empire. Judgment did indeed come
upon Babylon when it was absorbed by the Persians and
the once mighty kingdom simply ceased to exist. The genre
of prophetic judgment, however, does not demand a literal
fulfilment of every detail of its impressionistic terminology.
Such prophecy finds its fulfilment in the fact that judgment
does indeed take place. Similar examples of exaggeration
and hyperbole in prophetic judgments include Deuteronomy 28:25–46; Isaiah 3:24–4:1; 33:9; 34:1–15; Jeremiah
4:11–13, 23–26; 15:8; Amos 8:9; Nahum 1:4–5; Habakkuk
1:6–9; 3:10–12; and Zechariah 2:4–5. Another factor that
comes into play here is the fact that prophecies of judgment
were seen as a foreshadowing of the final eschatological
judgment which is to come. Each historical judgment was
understood as an adumbration of God's righteous outwork-
ing of his justice at the end of history.

Prophetic references to future blessings are also frequently
given in picturesque and exaggerated language. With regard
to Israel's return from exile the prophet Ezekiel uses the
eschatological language of resurrection:

The hand of the LORD was upon me, and he brought me
out by the Spirit of the LORD, and set me down in the midst
of the valley; it was full of bones. And he led me round
among them; and behold, there were very many upon the
valley; and lo, they were very dry. And he said to me, "Son
of man, can these bones live?" And I answered, "O Lord
GOD, thou knowest." Again he said to me, "Prophesy to
these bones and say to them, O dry bones, hear the word
of the LORD. Thus says the Lord GOD to these bones:

Behold, I will cause breath to enter you, and you shall live. And I will lay sinews upon you, and will cause flesh to come upon you, and cover you with skin, and put breath in you, and you shall live; and you shall know that I am the LORD.'' [Ezek. 37:1-6]

With regard to the messianic age, the Old Testament prophets frequently painted idyllic scenes in which the curse and hostilities of nature are undone:

The wolf shall dwell with the lamb, and the leopard shall lie down with the kid, and the calf and the lion and the fatling together, and a little child shall lead them. The cow and the bear shall feed; their young shall lie down together; and the lion shall eat straw like the ox. The sucking child shall play over the hole of the asp, and the weaned child shall put his hand on the adder's den. They shall not hurt or destroy in all my holy mountain; for the earth shall be full of the knowledge of the LORD as the waters cover the sea. [Isa. 11:6-9]

For waters shall break forth in the wilderness, and streams in the desert; the burning sand shall become a pool, and the thirsty ground springs of water; the haunt of jackals shall become a swamp, the grass shall become reeds and rushes. [Isa. 35:6b-7; see also 41:18-19]

For you shall go out in joy, and be led forth in peace; the mountains and the hills before you shall break forth into singing, and all the trees of the field shall clap their hands. Instead of the thorn shall come up the cypress; instead of the brier shall come up the myrtle; and it shall be to the LORD for a memorial, for an everlasting sign which shall not be cut off. [Isa. 55:12-13]

Regardless of how great a renewal occurred with the coming of the messianic age, it is clear that the mountains and hills did not sing, nor did trees clap their hands. (See also Isa. 35; 60:15-22; Mic. 4:4.)

That Jesus and the New Testament writers understood the prophetic literature to contain picturesque and exaggerated language is evident by the way they interpreted certain Old Testament prophecies. Whereas the main emphasis of a prophecy was usually interpreted in a literal fashion, there was also an awareness that not all of the portrait was to be interpreted literally. A good example is Joel 2:28–32:

> And it shall come to pass afterward, that I will pour out my spirit on all flesh; your sons and your daughters shall prophesy, your old men shall dream dreams, and your young men shall see visions. Even upon the menservants and maidservants in those days, I will pour out my spirit.
>
> And I will give portents in the heavens and on the earth, blood and fire and columns of smoke. The sun shall be turned to darkness, and the moon to blood, before the great and terrible day of the LORD comes. And it shall come to pass that all who call upon the name of the LORD shall be delivered; for in Mount Zion and in Jerusalem there shall be those who escape, as the LORD has said, and among the survivors shall be those whom the LORD calls.

In Acts 2:16 Peter states concerning the events of Pentecost that "this is what was spoken by the prophet Joel" and then proceeds to quote the passage. Apparently Peter (and/or Luke) understood that the astronomical terminology in the prophecy is not to be understood literally but indicates the eschatological nature of the coming of the Spirit and its inauguration of the new age. The nonliteral fulfilment of some of the details in Joel is quite disturbing to many readers. In fact some are so disturbed by this that they deny that the events of Pentecost are in fact the fulfilment (or complete fulfilment) of the prophecy. Not recognizing the impressionistic quality of prophetic language, they argue that what happened at Pentecost resembled what Joel prophesied but was not the actual fulfilment of his words. Yet surely Peter's understanding as recorded by Luke in Acts 2:16—"this is what was spoken by the prophet Joel"— means that the events of Pentecost are the fulfilment of what Joel prophesied.

A similar process is also at work in MARK 9:11–13. In reference to the prophecy in Malachi 4:5 that Elijah will come "before the great and terrible day of the LORD," Jesus is asked, "Why do the scribes say that first Elijah must come?" To this Jesus replies,

> Elijah does come first to restore all things; and how is it written of the Son of man, that he should suffer many things and be treated with contempt? But I tell you that Elijah has come, and they did to him whatever they pleased, as it is written of him.

Jesus maintains that although John the Baptist was not Elijah *redivivus* (John 1:19–23), he nonetheless was the fulfilment of the person and role portrayed in the prophecy of Malachi 4:5.

With this as a background we should not be surprised to find exaggeration in some of the prophetic sayings of Jesus, and indeed we do. Note the following examples:

> Do you see these great buildings? There will not be left here one stone upon another, that will not be thrown down. [MARK 13:2]

> You will be hated by all for my name's sake. [MARK 13:13a]

> But when you see the desolating sacrilege set up where it ought not to be (let the reader understand), then let those who are in Judea flee to the mountains; let him who is on the housetop not go down, nor enter his house, to take anything away; and let him who is in the field not turn back to take his mantle. [MARK 13:14–16]

> But in those days, after that tribulation, the sun will be darkened, and the moon will not give its light, and the stars will be falling from heaven, and the powers in the heavens will be shaken. [MARK 13:24–25]

> The queen of the South will arise at the judgment with the men of this generation and condemn them; for she came from the ends of the earth to hear the wisdom of Solomon, and behold, something greater than Solomon is here. The men of Nineveh will arise at the judgment with this genera-

tion and condemn it; for they repented at the preaching of
Jonah, and behold, something greater than Jonah is here.
[LUKE 11:31-32]

It has already been mentioned that the exaggerated nature
of MARK 13:2 is witnessed to by the fact that some of the
foundation stones of the Herodian temple still remain "one
stone upon another" even though the city and temple, in
fulfilment of Jesus' prophecy, were totally destroyed by the
Romans in A.D. 70.

As to MARK 13:13a we need not interpret the expression "hated by all" so narrowly as to infer that every one
of the earth's population will hate the followers of Christ.
A good indication of how this verse should be interpreted
can be gleaned from Acts 4. Here, after Peter and John are
released from prison, the church prays,

> Sovereign Lord, who didst make the heaven and the earth
> and the sea and everything in them, who by the mouth of
> our father David, thy servant, didst say by the Holy Spirit,
> "Why did the Gentiles rage, and the peoples imagine vain
> things? The kings of the earth set themselves in array, and
> the rulers were gathered together, against the Lord and
> against his Anointed"—for truly in this city there were
> gathered together against thy holy servant Jesus, whom
> thou didst anoint, both Herod and Pontius Pilate, with the
> Gentiles and the peoples of Israel, to do whatever thy hand
> and thy plan had predestined to take place. And now, Lord,
> look upon their threats, and grant to thy servants to speak
> thy word with all boldness, while thou stretchest out thy
> hand to heal, and signs and wonders are performed through
> the name of thy holy servant Jesus. [Acts 4:24-30]

The church quotes Psalm 2:1-2 to portray the animosity and
hostility of their enemies toward both their Lord and
themselves. In the prayer the enemies mentioned by the
psalmist (the Gentiles, the peoples, the kings of the earth,
and the rulers) are interpreted as being Herod, Pontius
Pilate, the Gentiles, and the peoples of Israel. The latter two
expressions of necessity include everyone on earth! Yet

those who prayed this prayer knew that there were some, themselves included, who had loved Jesus during his ministry. And they also knew that whereas the leadership of Israel opposed the church, the people in general did not (Acts 2:47; 5:13). What we have in Acts 4:24–30 and MARK 13:13a is the use of exaggerated language to stress the persecution and opposition that the church faced and faces. These passages do not describe with literal exactness the number of the enemies of the church; rather, they are impressionistic expressions of the intensity of the persecution and warnings that the future persecution of Christ's followers will indeed be severe.

The language of MARK 13:14–16 also appears to be exaggerated, for if this passage refers to the revolt of the Jewish nation and its destruction in A.D. 70, there certainly would have been time to enter one's house to grab one's mantle. The Roman legions at times moved swiftly but not that swiftly. (Actually the Roman legions tended to move rather slowly and methodically.) If, on the other hand, these verses refer to the great tribulation of the end times, would fleeing to the mountains of Judea do any good? Not at all! Furthermore, the Evangelists (parallel passages appear in Matthew and Luke), in writing for audiences who did not live in Palestine, knew that their readers would not interpret this warning literally. How could they (or we) flee to the mountains of Judea at the time of "the desolating sacrilege"? The very fact that the Gospel writers believed that these verses were meaningful for their non-Judean audiences indicates that they regarded them metaphorically as referring to a tribulation which would involve their non-Judean readers. Similarly, the astronomical language of MARK 13:24–25, a passage which speaks of the coming tribulation, may entail exaggeration as a consequence of its use of idiomatic eschatological terminology.

Finally, although it is not impossible that the queen of Sheba and the people of Nineveh will accuse the men of Jesus' generation on the great day of judgment (LUKE 11:31–32), it seems more likely that Jesus is declaring that if the queen of Sheba and the Ninevites acknowledged the presence of divine wisdom in, respectively, the words of Solomon and Jonah, how much more should his own audience acknowledge the divine message he proclaimed and respond accordingly!

Exaggeration in poetry

Another literary form or genre which frequently contains exaggeration is poetry. We even speak of poetic license or poetic heightening to describe the freedom of the poet to exaggerate. Because of the need for meter and/or rhyme, poets are permitted to use language more freely in order to express their thoughts. Furthermore, the very use of this genre indicates that the writer or speaker is not interested merely in the conveying of literal information; prose would be more conducive for that purpose. Rather, poetry is used to make an impression, to influence, to help people memorize ideas.

Biblical poetry is most readily recognized by the presence of parallelism or rhythmic balance. An expression coined to describe this phenomenon is *parallelismus membrorum* (parallelism in the members). Various types of parallelism can be found in the Bible: (1) synonymous parallelism—the succeeding line or lines repeat essentially the same thought in a balanced cadence but use different words; (2) antithetical parallelism—the second line expresses an opposite thought; (3) synthetic or constructive parallelism—the succeeding line or lines supplement or bring the thought of the first line to completion; (4) step parallelism—the second line advances the thought of the first line one additional step; and (5) chiasmic parallelism—the second line expresses the thought of the first line (or its antithesis) in inverted order (abba).

It should be pointed out that poetry does not require the use of exaggeration but rather is prone to it. Some Old Testament examples should be looked at first. We have already mentioned that proverbs incline toward exaggeration. One of the reasons for this is their frequent appearance in poetic form. Note for instance the following:

A wise son makes a glad father, but a foolish man despises his mother. [Prov. 15:20]

A tranquil mind gives life to the flesh, but passion makes the bones rot. [Prov. 14:30]

In the first instance "despises" does seem a rather exaggerated word, and in the latter "rot" is certainly not a literal description of what actually occurs; but we must remember that in these proverbs we are dealing with poetry, and exaggeration is quite common in this form of literature. In Malachi 1:2–3 two factors betray the presence of exaggeration. First, there is its rhythmic nature: "Yet I have loved Jacob but I have hated Esau." Second, there is the word *hated*. We have already suggested that on occasion "hate" does not mean "to bear malice toward someone," but "to love someone less than another." The idiomatic meaning of the term combines with poetic contrast to form an exaggerated statement which emphasizes God's gracious calling and the covenant which he established with Jacob. (The saying is only tangentially concerned with Esau.)

Contrasting the narrative account of the defeat of Sisera in Judges 4 with Deborah's poetic version in Judges 5 will give us a good idea of poetry's tendency to exaggerate. In the narrative account the battle and the death of Sisera are described in a straightforward manner. Deborah's song, however, is prone to exaggeration:

LORD, when thou didst go forth from Seir, when thou didst march from the region of Edom, the earth trembled, and the heavens dropped, yea, the clouds dropped water. The mountains quaked before the LORD, yon Sinai before the LORD, the God of Israel. . . . The kings came, they fought; then fought the kings of Canaan, at Taanach, by the waters of Megiddo; they got no spoils of silver. From heaven fought the stars, from their courses they fought against Sisera. [Judg. 5:4–5, 19–20]

In the past the poetic nature of this song was frequently ignored by the commentators, and various literal explanations of its assertions were offered (storms, earthquakes, hail). Recognition of the poetic nature of these verses, however, enables us to see that the singer is metaphorically proclaiming that God was with his people in battle and that through his power and might victory was won. We are not being told that the stars literally fought against Sisera.[19] (For a similar poetic description using cosmic terminology, see 2 Sam. 22:8–16, where God's deliverance of David from his enemies is depicted with great exaggeration.)

Still another example of the use of poetry to portray a historical incident in unusually picturesque language is found in Exodus 15. After a straightforward narration of Israel's safe passage through the Red Sea and the subsequent destruction of Pharaoh's armies (Exod. 14:21–29), the victory is described poetically. The metaphorical and exaggerated nature of the poetic version is immediately apparent:

> I will sing to the LORD, for he has triumphed gloriously; the horse and his rider he has thrown into the sea. . . . Pharaoh's chariots and his host he cast into the sea; and his picked officers are sunk in the Red Sea. . . . In the greatness of thy majesty thou overthrowest thy adversaries; thou sendest forth thy fury, it consumes them like stubble. . . .
>   Sing to the LORD, for he has triumphed gloriously; the horse and his rider he has thrown into the sea. [Exod. 15:1, 4, 7, 21]

Whereas the narrative account reports that the chariots of Pharaoh followed after Israel (14:23) and the waters came back over them (14:26–28), in the poetic version the Lord, who is seen as a mighty warrior (15:3), picks up his enemies and casts them into the sea (15:1, 4, 21). All the time, however, it is evident from 15:8–10 that the poet is aware of what actually happened: the waters which had been made to part for the children of Israel returned to cover the forces of Pharaoh. It is interesting to note that in the midst of the poem an entirely different metaphor is used to speak of the Lord's destruction of Pharaoh's armies, a metaphor which seems at first glance highly inappropriate. In 15:7b the destruction of Pharaoh's armies by drowning is likened to fire consuming stubble. Yet the poet is not troubled by the mixed figures. Remember that we are dealing with poetry and not historical narrative; both drowning and the burning of stubble are metaphors of judgment and destruction, and judgment and destruction did in fact come upon the armies of Pharaoh. (Still another example of the difference between the more sober nature of narrative and the more picturesque and exaggerated nature of poetry can be seen by comparing the creation narrative in Gen. 1 with its poetic counterpart in Ps. 104.)

Within the Gospels we find a large number of examples of poetry. By far the most numerous kind is antithetical parallelism; one author lists 138 instances in the Synoptic Gospels alone.[20] To these can be added about seventy-five cases of the four other kinds of parallelism.[21] Let us consider just a few examples of poetry in the teachings of Jesus:

> No one can serve two masters; for either he will hate the one and love the other, or he will be devoted to the one and despise the other. You cannot serve God and mammon. [MATT. 6:24]

> Ask, and it will be given you; seek, and you will find; knock, and it will be opened to you. For every one who asks receives, and he who seeks finds, and to him who knocks it will be opened. [MATT. 7:7–8]

> Do not think that I have come to bring peace on earth; I have not come to bring peace, but a sword. [MATT. 10:34]

Although there are other signals of exaggeration in all three of these examples, the fact that they are in poetic form is also a signal and may help explain in part the presence of exaggeration, for poetry is conducive to exaggeration. Other examples of exaggeration in the poetical utterances of Jesus include MATTHEW 5:39–41; Matthew 6:5–6; MARK 2:21–22; and Luke 16:10.[22]

Exaggeration in metaphor

Another literary form that must be mentioned is

metaphor. By its very nature metaphor involves exaggeration, for it does not say that something is like something else, which can be true, but that something is something else, which cannot be true. A simile is a comparison of two different things which is introduced by the word *like* or *as*. By the use of this introductory word, a simile avoids any absolute identification of the objects compared. A metaphor, on the other hand, is an absolute comparison of two unlike things, and this as a matter of course involves exaggeration. Consider the following examples:

> But I am a worm, and no man;
>   scorned by men, and despised by the people.
>   [Ps. 22:6; see also Ps. 102:3–11]

> I am a rose of Sharon,
>   a lily of the valleys. [Song of Sol. 2:1]

> There shall come forth a shoot from the stump of Jesse,
>   and a branch shall grow out of his roots. [Isa. 11:1]

> You are the salt of the earth; but if salt has lost its taste, how shall its saltness be restored? [MATT. 5:13]

> You serpents, you brood of vipers, how are you to escape being sentenced to hell? [Matt. 23:33]

> At that very hour some Pharisees came, and said to him, "Get away from here, for Herod wants to kill you." And he said to them, "Go and tell that fox, 'Behold, I cast out demons and perform cures today and tomorrow, and the third day I finish my course.' " [Luke 13:31–32]

In these examples it is evident that the persons referred to in the metaphor are not, respectively, a worm, a rose, a stump or branch, salt, vipers, or an actual fox. In one way or another they resemble the object used to describe them, but they are not identical with the object. We must be aware, then, that metaphors by their very nature entail exaggeration.

Exaggeration in *mashal*/parable

Closely related to two forms already mentioned, proverbs and metaphors, are the Old Testament *mashal* and its New Testament equivalent, the parable. Actually, under the term *mashal* or parable can be included not only proverb and metaphor, but also riddle, allegory, taunt, similitude, story and example parables.[23]

Exaggeration is commonplace within the Old Testament *mashal*. Consider, for example, Ezekiel 20:49–21:5:

> Then I said, "Ah Lord GOD! they are saying of me, 'Is he not a maker of allegories?' "
>
> The word of the LORD came to me: "Son of man, set your face toward Jerusalem and preach against the sanctuaries; prophesy against the land of Israel and say to the land of Israel, Thus says the LORD: Behold, I am against you, and will draw forth my sword out of its sheath, and will cut off from you both righteous and wicked. Because I will cut off from you both righteous and wicked, therefore my sword shall go out of its sheath against all flesh from south to north; and all flesh shall know that I the LORD have drawn my sword out of its sheath; it shall not be sheathed again.

Other examples of exaggeration in the Old Testament *mashal* are 2 Samuel 12:1–4; Isaiah 5:1–4; and Ezekiel 17; 24:2–5.

It is not surprising, then, that despite the real-life and down-to-earth nature of Jesus' parables we frequently encounter exaggeration in them. To be sure, the parables are not fablelike in quality, for trees and animals do not talk and people do not fly, but the parables nevertheless do use exaggerated language. A good example is the parable of the unforgiving servant:

> Therefore the kingdom of heaven may be compared to a king who wished to settle accounts with his servants. When he began the reckoning, one was brought to him who owed him ten thousand talents; and as he could not pay, his lord ordered him to be sold, with his wife and children and all that he had, and payment to be made. So the servant fell

on his knees, imploring him, "Lord, have patience with me, and I will pay you everything." And out of pity for him the lord of that servant released him and forgave him the debt. But that same servant, as he went out, came upon one of his fellow servants who owed him a hundred denarii; and seizing him by the throat he said, "Pay what you owe." So his fellow servant fell down and besought him, "Have patience with me, and I will pay you." He refused and went and put him in prison till he should pay the debt. When his fellow servants saw what had taken place, they were greatly distressed, and they went and reported to their lord all that had taken place. Then his lord summoned him and said to him, "You wicked servant! I forgave you all that debt because you besought me; and should not you have had mercy on your fellow servant, as I had mercy on you?" And in anger his lord delivered him to the jailers, till he should pay all his debt. So also my heavenly Father will do to every one of you, if you do not forgive your brother from your heart. [Matt. 18:23–35]

The exaggerated nature of this parable is apparent in the huge sum which the unforgiving servant was forgiven. It was 10,000 talents. In comparison, the entire tribute of Galilee and Perea for 4 B.C. was only 200 talents and the entire yearly income of Herod the Great was only 900 talents![24]

Other examples can also be listed. Is it not strange that all ten maidens were asleep when the bridegroom came (Matt. 25:5)? And is it not strange that all those invited to the banquet made excuses and did not attend (LUKE 14:18)? And certainly not all Samaritans were as good as the one in the story or all priests and Levites as bad (Luke 10:30–35). As for the rich man who forgave the dishonest steward (Luke 16:1–9), surely his behavior was quite unusual; and, alas, fathers like the father of the prodigal son are all too rare (Luke 15:11–32). Although of a real-life quality, the parabolic form by its very nature permits and even encourages the unusual and the exaggerated, for we are not dealing here with history but story!

In concluding our discussion of the various literary forms which are prone to exaggeration and which should therefore alert us to the possibility of hyperbolic language, it should be pointed out that these forms (except for metaphor) do not inevitably contain exaggeration. Some instances of these forms contain exaggeration and some do not. Each individual example must be examined in the light of all the canons which we are discussing in this volume. It should also be pointed out that whereas one may take exception as to whether a specific example we have given does indeed contain exaggeration, we have in the case of each canon presented a sufficient number of other examples to warrant regarding it as a signal of possible exaggeration.

CANON 11. A statement which uses idiomatic language may contain exaggeration

It is a characteristic of every language that certain terms and phrases become part of a storehouse of idioms whose meaning is no longer determined by their literal sense and grammatical relationships, but rather by the way they are used and function in everyday speech. One of the greatest problems in learning a new language is the existence of idioms. Beginners always stumble over this problem, for what seems like a harmless statement in the new language may turn out to be idiomatic and have nuances that can be quite embarrassing. For example, to translate into German a simple statement of how one is being affected by the temperature can be disastrous. The English "I am hot" cannot be literally translated "Ich bin heiss," but must be translated "Mir ist es heiss" (i.e., "to me it is hot"), for whereas the latter German sentence refers to the temperature, the former is idiomatic and actually refers to sexual temperature (arousal)!

In English we use idioms all the time to express ideas and thoughts which are quite different from the literal meaning of the individual words and the grammatical construction. "Have a good day" is not literally a command which the hearer is to obey, but a simple farewell. "How are you?"

many times is simply a greeting; often the last thing the speaker wants to hear is how the person really is. Even an atheist will use the idiom "God bless you," which for him is equivalent to the idiom "Gesundheit" (literally, "good health"). Some idioms exaggerate in order to describe certain feelings: "If I don't get something cold to drink, I'll die of thirst"; "If that happened to me, I would be embarrassed to death"; "His best friend kicked the bucket"; "Yesterday when I went shopping, I just ran around in circles"; "She's really gone off the deep end"; "He must have eyes in the back of his head." These are all idioms whose meanings today have little correlation with the precise grammatical relationships and the literal meanings of the terms employed. Furthermore, there appears to be in all cultures a host of universal archetypal symbols which quickly take on idiomatic significance: fire, water, bread, light, darkness, blood, up, down, plowing, reaping, washing.

In interpreting the teachings of Jesus, as well as all literature and speech, it is therefore clear that we must be alert to the use of idiomatic language. To complicate the matter even further we must be aware that the meanings of idioms are not static but fluid. They change. This is especially true in our society and time. In the past, to be described as "square" was a compliment; today it is an insult! We must, then, make sure to interpret a biblical idiom in light of its meaning at the time it was written. Fortunately, drastic changes in meanings were far less frequent in ancient societies than they are today. Nevertheless, the root definition of terms (i.e., their etymology) may be of little significance in seeking to understand the meaning of a phrase, for what is needed is not a knowledge of the history of the terms found therein, but rather a knowledge of the usage of the phrase at the time it was written or uttered. (To use more technical terminology, we are primarily interested in the synchronic dimension of a term rather than its diachronic evolution.)

Within the Old Testament we find a number of terms and phrases which, interpreted literally, mean something totally different from what they meant in actual practice and usage. Some of these idioms use exaggerated language. A good example is the love-hate antithesis:

> If a man have two wives, one beloved, and another hated, and they have born him children, both the beloved and the hated; and if the firstborn son be hers that was hated: Then it shall be, when he maketh his sons to inherit that which he hath, that he may not make the son of the beloved firstborn before the son of the hated, which is indeed the firstborn: But he shall acknowledge the son of the hated for the firstborn, by giving him a double portion of all that he hath: for he is the beginning of his strength; the right of the firstborn is his. [Deut. 21:15–17, KJV]

> "I have loved you," says the LORD. But you say, "How hast thou loved us?" "Is not Esau Jacob's brother?" says the LORD. "Yet I have loved Jacob but I have hated Esau; I have laid waste his hill country and left his heritage to jackals of the desert." [Mal. 1:2–3]

In both these references the idiomatic love-hate antithesis actually signifies a contrast between loving more and loving less. In the Deuteronomic passage what we have is not an absolute love for one wife and an absolute hatred for the other, but rather a favoring of the one wife over the other. In fact, the Hebrew word which the King James renders "hate," the Revised Standard renders "dislike." Two other examples of this idiom are 2 Samuel 19:6 (v. 7 in the Hebrew text) and Proverbs 13:24. The true nature of this idiom is perhaps most apparent in Genesis 29:30–31:

> So Jacob went in to Rachel also, and he loved Rachel more than Leah, and served Laban for another seven years. When the LORD saw that Leah was hated, he opened her womb; but Rachel was barren.

Here it is clear that Leah's being hated (v. 31) does not mean that Jacob was malevolent or harbored malice toward her. What it means is that Jacob loved Rachel more than Leah (v. 30), that is, he loved Leah less. (In the poetry of the ancient Near East numerous terms were paired together. In such instances the meaning of these terms is far more dependent upon their idiomatic usage together than upon their literal meaning in isolation.)[25]

An idiom frequently used to express the loss of courage is the figure of a melting heart (Josh. 2:11; 5:1; 7:5; 2 Sam. 17:10; Ps. 112:10). Here a literal interpreting of the idiom would, of course, be absurd.

Over the centuries many Christians have been offended by Psalm 137:8-9 because they have not understood its idiomatic nature:

> O daughter of Babylon, you devastator!
>   Happy shall he be who requites you
>   with what you have done to us!
> Happy shall he be who takes your little ones
>   and dashes them against the rock![26]

How could the psalmist wish such terrible and hateful revenge upon the Babylonian children? How could such verses be included in the Scriptures? Once we realize, however, that what we have in this passage is an idiomatic picture of divine retribution and judgment upon an evil nation for their sins, much of the problem disappears. What the psalmist is seeking is not an actual smashing of Babylonian children against the rocks, but rather an earthly manifestation of divine judgment through which God will demonstrate his righteousness. The reference is not meant to be taken literally, but is to be understood as idiomatic language for the establishment of divine judgment and righteousness upon the earth.[27] If these verses are understood in this way, their seeming offensiveness disappears.

Some areas have their own special cluster of idioms. For instance, a number of idiomatic phrases are associated with the theme of judgment, the horror of the divine wrath. The same idioms are used for the temporal chastenings of Israel, Judah, and other biblical nations, and for the final judgment which will occur at the end of history.[28] We read that the sun will no longer give its light (Isa. 13:10; 24:23; Ezek. 32:7-8; Joel 2:10, 31; 3:15; Amos 8:9). We read of earthquakes (Zech. 14:5; 2 Baruch 27:7; 70:8; 2 Esdras 9:3), of fire (2 Baruch 27:10; 70:8; 2 Esdras 5:8), of drought (1 Enoch 80:2), of famine and sword and pestilence (Jer. 11:22; 14:12; 16:4; 21:9; Ezek. 6:11). We read that the land will become a wilderness (Isa. 64:10; Jer. 9:12; 23:10; Joel 2:3). Of course some of these figures (e.g., fire, famine, sword, and pestilence) are naturally associated with war and siege, but as time progressed they came to be associated with virtually any type of judgment.

In a similar manner the themes of future deliverance from one's enemies and the blessing and bliss of the new age also have their cluster of idioms. We read, for example, that the lamb and the wolf (or lion) will exist side by side (Isa. 11:6–9; 65:25) and that the wilderness and desert will turn into forests and fruitful fields where water abounds (Isa. 32:15; 35:1, 6–7; 41:18–19; 43:19–20). The promise made to Abraham that his seed will be as numerous as the sand of the sea is yet another common idiomatic exaggeration (Gen. 22:17; cf. 32:12; Josh. 11:4; Judg. 7:12).

It is not surprising, then, to find in Jesus' teaching concerning the judgment to come similar idiomatic language:

> For nation will rise against nation, and kingdom against kingdom; there will be earthquake in various places, there will be famines; this is but the beginning of the sufferings. [MARK 13:8]

> But in those days, after that tribulation, the sun will be darkened, and the moon will not give its light, and the stars will be falling from heaven, and the powers in the heaven will be shaken. [MARK 13:24–25]

> The Son of man will send his angels, and they will gather out of his kingdom all causes of sin and all evildoers, and throw them into the furnace of fire; there men will weep and gnash their teeth. [Matt. 13:41–42]

> So it will be at the close of the age. The angels will come out and separate the evil from the righteous, and throw them into the furnace of fire; there men will weep and gnash their teeth. [Matt. 13:49–50]

And cast the worthless servant into the outer darkness; there men will weep and gnash their teeth. [Matt. 25:30]

The idiomatic nature of the terminology in MARK 13:8 and 24–25 is quite apparent from the Old Testament references already given. "To weep and gnash the teeth" is a favorite expression of Matthew (8:12; 13:42, 50; 22:13; 24:51; 25:30). Although the same combination is found elsewhere only in LUKE 13:28, the expression "to gnash one's teeth" was a common idiom for rage, mockery, or pain (Job 16:9; Pss. 35:16; 37:12; 112:10; Lam. 2:16; Acts 7:54). That "the furnace of fire [hell]" had also become an idiom by New Testament times is evident from 2 Esdras 7:36; 1 Enoch 10:13; and 4 Maccabees 16:21.

There are other exaggerations which appear to be idiomatic: a camel going through the eye of a needle (MARK 10:25; cf. b. Berachoth 55b; b. Baba Metzia 38b) and faith which can remove mountains (MATT. 17:20; 21:21; 1 Cor. 13:2) or cast a tree into the sea (Luke 17:5–6). If we are correct in claiming that these are idioms, the hearers of Jesus would no more have interpreted them literally than we would interpret a reference to "Rev. Jones's faith which can remove mountains" literally. The faith which can remove mountains is great faith in God, not an ability to eliminate Mount Everest from the face of the earth. Once we become aware of the presence of idioms in the teachings of Jesus, we should be on guard not to interpret them literally.

CANON 12. A statement which uses universal language may contain exaggeration

The presence of universal language in a statement is also an indication that the saying may be an exaggeration. In everyday speech we frequently use universal language to express general truths, yet for such statements there will almost always be exceptions. We have already noted this in regard to proverbs. Some people, however, believe that a universal or all-inclusive statement is by definition an exaggeration. They are wrong, for there are, of course, all-inclusive statements that are literally true. When Paul says, "All have sinned and fall short of the glory of God" (Rom. 3:23), he is literally correct. All in Adam have sinned. There is none righteous, no, not one (Rom. 3:10).[29] Similarly, Paul intends for his readers to take the universal statement in 2 Corinthians 5:10 literally: "For we must all appear before the judgment seat of Christ, so that each one may receive good or evil, according to what he has done in the body." Jesus also makes universal statements which must be taken in a literal way. There is no trace of exaggeration when he says, "Unless you repent you will all likewise perish" (Luke 13:3, 5).

Nevertheless, it is more often true than not that unqualified general propositions found in the Bible are exaggerated statements.[30] There are numerous instances where Jesus used universal language in ways which make it clear that he did not intend for his words to be interpreted literally. Instead he intended that the all-inclusive language be understood as making his basic point all the more emphatic. There are many precedents in the Old Testament; the writers expected their audience to understand that some of their universal statements were not to be taken literally.[31] Consider, for example, Jeremiah 6:13, where the prophet condemns the corruption in Judah:

> For from the least to the greatest of them, every one is greedy for unjust gain; and from prophet to priest, every one deals falsely.

Surely Jeremiah is not claiming that there is not a single priest or prophet who is not greedy and does not deal falsely. After all, he himself is a prophet!

It is not surprising, then, that Jesus uses universal language in a similar way:

> And Jesus said to him, "If you can! All things are possible to him who believes." [Mark 9:23]

> Give to every one who begs from you; and of him who takes away your goods, do not ask them again. [LUKE 6:30]

But woe to you, scribes and Pharisees, hypocrites! Because you shut the kingdom of heaven against men; for you neither enter yourself, nor allow those who would enter to go in. [MATT. 23:13]

Are all things indeed possible to him who believes? Is the believer really omnipotent? Surely many qualifiers are assumed in Mark 9:23. The believer cannot become God nor cause God to cease existing. The believer cannot violate the laws of logic, and in particular the law of contradiction, nor change the fate of the dead. It is also clear from the teachings of Scripture that we should not give to every person who begs from us, for Paul in 2 Thessalonians 3:6–13 forbids giving to lazy Christians who refuse to earn their own living. Furthermore, every parent knows it is his duty at times not to give his children what they ask. Not only common sense but love demands this. Nevertheless, such exceptions should not lessen the impact of Jesus' teaching in LUKE 6:30: the believer is to be generous to the point of giving up all his goods, if God so wills. In the reference to the Pharisees and scribes in MATTHEW 23:13 we see another use of all-inclusive language, but certainly not every Pharisee and scribe was like the hypocrites described here and in MATTHEW 23:5–7, 23, 27, 29–30; Matthew 23:15, 24. After all, Nicodemus was a Pharisee (John 3:1), and in Luke 13:31 we read of certain Pharisees who warned Jesus of the danger posed by Herod. Yet a large number of Pharisees were hypocrites, so that Jesus in his rebuke of them could justifiably use all-inclusive language. Any Pharisee present could have profited from the warning and rebuke of Jesus, even as any American tourist can profit from the rebuke and castigation of all American tourists as ugly Americans. Such a rebuke makes those Americans who are a credit to their country all the more determined not to be ugly Americans. Other passages where Jesus' use of universal language is to be interpreted as exaggeration include MATTHEW 10:32 (cf. 7:21–22); 23:35; Matthew 23:3; MARK 2:21–22; 10:11–12; 13:30; and Luke 5:39.

CANON 13. A statement which deals with subject matter prone to exaggeration may contain exaggeration

Within the biblical materials, as well as in life in general, there are a number of subject areas which characteristically involve the use of exaggeration. We shall mention and illustrate only a few of them. One such area is descriptions of a person's emotional disposition. The Semite was certainly not one to hide feelings of misery or grief but expressed them openly for all to know.

My flesh is clothed with worms and dirt; my skin hardens, then breaks out afresh. My days are swifter than a weaver's shuttle and come to their end without hope. [Job 7:5–6]

I am weary with my moaning; every night I flood my bed with tears; I drench my couch with my weeping. My eye wastes away because of grief, it grows weak because of all my foes. [Ps. 6:6–7]

The exaggeration present in these examples is most apparent. Job's flesh was surely not covered with worms, nor did his days pass as quickly as a weaver handles a shuttle. As for the psalmist, it is doubtful that his tears flooded his bed and that his grief caused his eye to waste away (literally, to be moth-eaten). Similar examples of exaggeration to express grief and misery can be found in Job 6:2–4; 9:17–18; 16:11–16; Psalms 22; 38; 69; 88:3–9; 102:3–11; Isaiah 21:3–4; and Lamentations 3:1–21. To these Old Testament examples we can add Jesus' words in Gethsemane:

And he said to them, "My soul is very sorrowful, even to death." [MARK 14:34]

Another area in which we frequently encounter the use of exaggeration is promises or words of encouragement. Note, for instance, how God encouraged Abraham and his descendants:

I will make your descendants as the dust of the earth; so

that if one can count the dust of the earth, your descendants also can be counted. [Gen. 13:16]

"Look toward heaven, and number the stars, if you are able to number them." Then he said to him, "So shall your descendants be." [Gen. 15:5]

I will do you good, and make your descendants as the sand of the sea, which cannot be numbered for multitude. [Gen. 32:12]

One need only reflect upon the impossibility of counting the dust of the earth, the stars, and the sand of the sea to see the exaggerated nature of these promises. Consider also God's description of the Promised Land into which Moses would lead the people of Israel:

Then the LORD said, "I have seen the affliction of my people who are in Egypt, and have heard their cry because of their taskmasters; I know their sufferings, and I have come down to deliver them out of the hand of the Egyptians, and to bring them up out of that land to a good and broad land, a land flowing with milk and honey, to the place of the Canaanites, the Hittites, the Amorites, the Perizzites, the Hivites, and the Jebusites. . . . I promise that I will bring you up out of the affliction of Egypt, to the land of the Canaanites, the Hittites, the Amorites, the Perizzites, the Hivites, and the Jebusites, a land flowing with milk and honey." [Exod. 3:7-8, 17]

Closely related to these promises are the numerous prophetic passages which in extravagant terminology encourage Israel with hopes of cosmic renewal as well as of judgment for her oppressors.[32] It is not surprising, therefore, to find that Jesus also used exaggeration as a means of encouragement for his disciples and as a medium for the divine promises:

But even the hairs of your head are all numbered. [MATT. 10:30]

Behold, I have given you authority to tread upon serpents

and scorpions, and over all the power of the enemy; and nothing shall hurt you. [Luke 10:19]

Among other passages that could be mentioned are MATTHEW 6:33; MARK 10:29–30; and LUKE 17:5–6.

Other areas could be named as well, for we often find exaggeration in passages containing numbers (Gen. 24:60; Exod. 1:7–9; Num. 10:36; Judg. 7:12; Ps. 3:6; 144:13), descriptions of size (Gen. 11:4; Deut. 1:28), or praise for heroes (Judg. 20:16; 2 Sam. 1:23). The reader of Scripture should keep in mind the almost universal tendency to exaggerate in such matters.

In concluding this chapter it will be profitable to comment in general on the various canons that have been discussed. Not all the canons listed are of equal value, and not every canon is applicable in every instance. Certain canons are, furthermore, less accessible to most readers of the Gospels. Most lay persons will find it more difficult to ascertain if a saying contains idiomatic language (canon 11) than to check if other sayings of Jesus contradict the literal meaning of the saying in question (canon 2). The following clues to the possible presence of exaggeration would appear to be serviceable for people with an elementary biblical understanding and a few minimal tools such as a Bible dictionary and concordance:

1. Statements which are literally impossible.
2. Statements which conflict with what Jesus says elsewhere.
3. Statements which conflict with the behavior and actions of Jesus elsewhere.
4. Statements which conflict with the teachings of the Old Testament.
5. Statements which conflict with the teachings of the New Testament.
7. Statements which the audience of Jesus did not interpret literally.
8. Statements which have not been fulfilled literally.
9. Statements which, if literally fulfilled, would not achieve the desired goal.

12. Statements which use universal language.

The remaining canons are more technical in nature and are accessible primarily to people with theological training:

6. Statements which are interpreted by another Evangelist in a nonliteral way.
10. Statements which use particular literary forms prone to exaggeration.
11. Statements which use idiomatic language.
13. Statements which deal with subject matter prone to exaggeration.

Notes

1. Other passages which picture the worm as an agent of judgment include Deut. 28:39 and Isa. 51:8. For unquenchable fire see Isa. 34:10; Jer. 7:20; 17:27; Ezek. 20:47–48.

2. MATT. 5:48 should be compared with its entire context and the parallel in LUKE 6:36.

3. August Tholuck, *Commentary on the Sermon on the Mount*, trans. R. Lundin Brown (Edinburgh: T. & T. Clark, 1860), p. 164, states, ''The correctness of the interpretation of a sentence and an isolated clause must be determined by the consistency of that interpretation with the idea of the whole work.''

4. Teachers do, of course, change their minds at times, but in such instances the teacher is under obligation to make clear to his pupils that what he says now should not be interpreted in the light of the previous context.

5. Claude C. Douglas, *Overstatement in the New Testament* (New York: Henry Holt, 1931), p. 90, rightly states, ''Either we must admit that here [Matt. 23:2–3] Jesus greatly exaggerates the facts or else he contradicts himself.''

6. That the antitheses in Matthew were not understood by the Evangelist as doing away with the teachings of the Old Testament is evident from the context. The antitheses must be interpreted in the light of Matt. 5:17–20. Here Jesus states that he has not come to destroy the Old Testament (''the law and the prophets'') but to fulfil it. To relax even one of the least important of its commandments is to make oneself least in the kingdom of heaven.

7. C. S. Lewis, *Fern-seed and Elephants and Other Essays on Christianity* (Glasgow: William Collins Sons, 1975), p. 112.

8. Tholuck, *Sermon on the Mount*, p. 165. Chrysostom's twenty-third homily on the Sermon on the Mount is still profitable reading for a proper interpretation of MATT. 7:1.

9. In 1 Cor. 7:10 Paul's words, "To the married I give charge, not I but the Lord," are best understood as referring not to a revelation from the risen Lord, but to a teaching of the historical Jesus. On the other hand, the material in vv. 12–13 is a revelation from the risen Lord ("To the rest I say, not the Lord," is to be understood in the light of 1 Cor. 7:40b—"And I think that I have the Spirit of God").

10. The present writer remembers a somewhat similar incident in his own life when he, for emphasis, also used exaggeration to present his view. In a discussion of situation ethics various individuals were speculating as to when it is all right to engage in sexual activity with someone other than one's spouse. All sorts of different hypothetical situations were being suggested, some of them extremely unrealistic and unlikely. Lost in the discussion were the divine rule and normal, usual situations. When asked my views, I responded that there is never a right occasion for adultery. Now hypothetically there might be an occasion when adultery is the lesser of two evils, but my concern was to bring the discussion back to the plan and purpose of sex as God has ordained it. As a result I gave the universal divine rule which is applicable at least 99.99999 percent of the time. I can easily see why Jesus reacted in a similar manner to a debate on acceptable reasons for divorce.

11. Compare here Rom. 3:6, where Paul argues that God must be just since he will judge the world. The certainty of this fact (God's judgment of the world) proved for Paul that God is just.

12. The very fact that Christians accept the truth of both MATT. 7:7–8 and James 4:3 indicates that they understand the former to be an overstatement. Qualifying a statement in any way indicates that we believe that statement to be an exaggeration. Any statement which we accept on the assumption of certain unstated qualifications is by definition an exaggeration.

13. G. B. Caird, *The Language and Imagery of the Bible* (Philadelphia: Westminister, 1980), p. 57, correctly points out that "it is characteristic of Semitic style to express ideas absolutely and to leave the listener to fill in for himself the implicit qualifications."

14. Origen *On First Principles* 4. 18.

15. Douglas, *Overstatement*, p. xiv.

16. Walter C. Kaiser, Jr., *Toward an Exegetical Theology* (Grand Rapids: Baker, 1981), p. 230, states concerning proverbs, "It is the nature of proverbial speech to assume that *ceteris paribus* ('all other things being equal'), this then is true."

17. For our purposes we shall not make any distinction between prophecy and apocalyptic literature.

18. Caird, *Language and Imagery*, pp. 56–57.

19. That the poet was aware of the actual facts is evident from 5:26 (cf. 4:21).

20. Joachim Jeremias, *New Testament Theology*, trans. John Bowden (New York: Scribner, 1971), pp. 15–16.

21. Robert H. Stein, *The Method and Message of Jesus' Teachings* (Philadelphia: Westminster, 1978), pp. 27–32.

22. Recognition of the exaggerated nature of poetry may also be helpful for understanding some of the pre-Pauline hymns. The hymnic nature of Col. 1:15–20 is generally conceded by all Pauline scholars. Is it possible that the universal quality of this hymn ("to reconcile to himself all things") is due more to the exaggerated nature of poetry than to an attempt to teach a universal salvation? Compare 1 Cor. 15:22, which at first glance also seems universalistic but must be interpreted in the light of the next verse, which speaks of "those who belong to Christ."

23. For a discussion of both the difficulty involved in defining a parable and the kinds of material that fall under its domain see Robert H. Stein, *An Introduction to the Parables of Jesus* (Philadelphia: Westminster, 1981), pp. 15–21.

24. Josephus *Antiquities of the Jews* 17. 318.

25. For examples of paired terms see Mitchell Dahood, "Ugaritic-Hebrew Parallel Pairs," in *Ras Shamra Parallels*, ed. Loren R. Fisher, Analecta Orientalia 49 (Rome: Pontificium Institutum Biblicum, 1972), vol. 1, pp. 71–382; Peter C. Craigie, "Parallel Word Pairs in the Song of Deborah (Judges 5)," *Journal of the Evangelical Theological Society* 20 (1977): 15–22.

26. See also Isa. 13:16; Hos. 10:14; 13:16; and Nah. 3:10, where, however, a different Hebrew verb is used.

27. Othmar Keel, *The Symbolism of the Biblical World*, trans. Timothy J. Hallett (New York: Seabury, 1978), p. 9. Keel points out that the reference to the destruction of the children, who "concretize the continuation of the unrighteous kingdom," should be understood as a figure symbolizing the complete destruction of that kingdom. Keel includes two illustrations (plates 341 and 342) of a ruler sitting on a throne and holding his son on his lap. Subject peoples are depicted beneath the *child's* feet. Dashing little ones against the rock, then, suggests the total destruction of Babylonian rule: both ruler and heir encounter divine judgment.

28. Cf. the description of the judgment of Babylon in Isaiah 13 with the specific historical circumstances. Some of the language used is clearly nonliteral and eschatological. See especially vv. 9–10, 13.

29. To pose Jesus as an exception here is to lose sight of the context of Rom. 3. Paul is referring to all flesh (Rom. 3:20), i.e., all who are in Adam (Rom. 5:12), both Jews and Greeks. He does not include Jesus among those who are in Adam. Note carefully the wording of Rom. 8:3: the Son did not come "in sinful flesh," but "in the likeness of sinful flesh." It is clear that, in Paul's view, Jesus Christ was sinless (2 Cor. 5:21).

30. The number of such universal statements in the Bible should be noted. Douglas, *Overstatement*, p. 7, states that the term *all* is used 5500+ times in the Bible; and when we add such terms as "any," "none," and "every," the number swells to over ten thousand!

31. See note 13.

32. See pp. 61–63.

3

The Purposes of Exaggerated Language

In chapter 1 of this volume we sought to demonstrate the presence of exaggerated language in the teachings of Jesus. We then sought in chapter 2 to establish certain canons by which such exaggeration can be detected. We listed thirteen canons and gave examples of how they can be used to detect exaggeration in Jesus' teachings and, for illustrative purposes, in the literature of the Old Testament as well. It is now time to deal with the function of exaggeration in literature in general and in the teachings of Jesus in particular.

The various kinds of language

The purpose of language varies according to the intention of the speaker or writer. One may, for instance, use language to instruct, to reason, to command, to stimulate, or to express feelings. To put it simply, we might say that language is essentially either referential or "commissive" in nature.[1] The primary aim of referential language is description. It seeks to convey and clarify information. In so doing it seeks to bring about a rational thinking process; it is more concerned with one's reason than with one's emotions. As a result it tends to be characterized by nonemotive or "steno-" words rather than "depth" or "tensive" words. Commissive language, on the other hand, seeks to cause things to happen (i.e., to persuade one to perform and do certain tasks rather than simply to inform of certain facts) or to elicit certain feelings. Commissive language seeks primarily to affect the hearer rather than to provide him with information. As a result it tends to be characterized by tensive and emotive words which challenge and bring about decision and empathy. It needs to be pointed out, however, that even as referential language, while conveying information to the mind, may also affect the emotions, so also commissive language, while seeking to affect the emotions, may at the same time convey information to the mind. The difference is one of emphasis. The prime goal of referential language is to convey information; the prime goal of commissive language is to affect the hearer's emotions.

Referential language tends to be literal and cognitive in nature and to take the form of declarative sentences. It appeals primarily to the mind and the thought processes. At times it intentionally refrains from the use of any terminology which may arouse the emotions, for it wants the recipient to think clearly and objectively. In order to realize this goal, it seeks to get rid of all ambiguity and achieve semantic precision.[2] As a result it may merely present the facts and nothing but the facts. An example of referential language is Dr. Robert H. Stone's letter to Dr. Anderson (p. 14). In this letter Dr. Stone used referential language as devoid of emotive terminology as was possible. It is, of course, debatable whether any communication can be completely free of emotional language. Certainly the description of the patient's heart condition would raise some emotional response from the patient. ''Paroxysmal atrial tachycardia'' can be a very emotional term even if the patient does not understand precisely what it entails. Naked facts can and frequently do stir emotions. A report on what transpired at Auschwitz may use only the sterile referential language of historiography, but the information conveyed will stir the emotions of the reader and result in a definite response. A straightforward presentation of pure facts can at times challenge, stir emotion, and bring about action. The reason for this is that certain information, even if presented in noncommissive language, will, upon encountering a related need or attitude in the individual, produce an affect of one sort or another. The facts of the gospel, even when presented in referential language, are nevertheless "the power of God for salvation" (Rom. 1:16). Referential language, however, has as its primary goal the conveying of information. It can therefore be evaluated as either true or false, because the information conveyed either corresponds to reality or it does not.

Commissive language, on the other hand, while it also conveys information, seeks not merely or principally to inform, but to affect the recipient in some way. One type of commissive language—"performative"—seeks in particular to effect some sort of performance from the hearer. In seeking to bring about performance, it frequently makes use of commands or imperatival sentences. Such commissive language seeks to get something done and carries with it a demand for decision and response. In seeking to achieve this aim, persuasive, emotional, and exaggerated language is frequently used, for such language has the capacity to stir the emotions. Of course we cannot evaluate the command itself as being true or false; rather, it must be evaluated as to whether it is valid or invalid in the light of our presuppositions. Performative language, then, seeks not so much to *de*scribe, but to *pre*scribe and bring about a response.

Another kind of commissive language—expressive—seeks to state certain facts in ways that will elicit specific feelings and attitudes. We saw an example in Dr. Stone's letter to Joan (p. 14). Here Dr. Stone not only sought to convey certain information (his love for Joan), but also to arouse her emotions by the use of exaggerated language. A bare, factual usage of referential language could not convey the feelings of Dr. Stone nearly as well as his use of figurative and exaggerated language. By the use of such language he sought not merely to convey to Joan knowledge and information concerning his attitude toward her, but also to communicate his feelings, his longings, his deep love for her as well. No doubt he also hoped that his choice of language would so affect Joan that she would respond towards him in kind. Language which seeks to make an impression frequently takes on poetic or metaphorical form. Like performative language, expressive language cannot usually be judged as being either true or false. A different evaluative description is required; for example, adequate or inadequate, effective or ineffective. There is a sense, however, in which expressive language can be judged to be true or false. If a speaker or writer is purposely deceitful and uses expressive language to mislead, then it would seem reasonable to conclude that the language is not merely inadequate or ineffective, but false as well. It does not truly express one's feelings or attitudes. If Dr. Stone loved Joan and expressed his love poorly, we might say that his language was inadequate and ineffective; but if he did not love Joan at all, his language was false.

In the teachings of Jesus we find all the forms of language we have just discussed. We find referential language in the places where Jesus is seeking primarily to convey information and to appeal to reason. A good example is MARK 3:22–27:

> And the scribes who came down from Jerusalem said, "He is possessed by Beelzebul, and by the prince of demons he casts out the demon." And he called them to him, and said to them in parables, "How can Satan cast out Satan? If a kingdom is divided against itself, that kingdom cannot stand. And if a house is divided against itself, that house will not be able to stand. And if Satan has risen up against himself and is divided, he cannot stand, but is coming to an end. But no one can enter a strong man's house and plunder his goods, unless he first binds the strong man; then indeed he may plunder his house."

In this passage Jesus clearly sought to reason with his opponents. Now it is of course true that Jesus was seeking ultimately some sort of a response from them and was not seeking here only to convey bare facts and to demonstrate a sterile, unemotional logic. Few religious teachers are ambivalent as to whether their students respond to what they are saying. Jesus always hoped for a positive response to everything he said and did. Here, however, the primary purpose of his language was to convey certain information and logical reasoning in a way which would appeal to his listeners' rational processes, to their minds rather than to their hearts. Other examples in which the referential dimension is dominant in the teachings of Jesus can be found in MARK 8:31; 9:9-13; 12:18-27, 28-34, 41-44; and Luke 17:20-21.

On the other hand, there are many instances in which Jesus' language was primarily performative. By nature every command or imperative is basically performative in function. Unless a command has become an idiom, it seeks to cause something to happen. "Have a good day" and "Enjoy yourself," although imperatival in form, no longer seek a response, but are simply idiomatic expressions for "Goodbye" (which itself is, literally, a contraction of "God be with you" and a simple idiom used at times of departure). Jesus issued a great number of commands, some explicit, some merely implied. True, many of them do not contain exaggeration. The commands to repent (MARK 1:15), to keep his words (MATT. 7:24-27), and to believe (MARK 1:15; John 14:1) are unadorned by exaggerated terminology. Yet on numerous occasions Jesus heightened the affective nature of his commands by using exaggeration. The commands to hate father and mother (LUKE 14:26), to cut off one's hand and pluck out one's eye (MARK 9:43-47), to refrain from judging (MATT. 7:1) and swearing (Matt. 5:34), all contain exaggerated language which serves to startle the hearer and make him reflect on the nature of Jesus' command and the performance demanded.

At times Jesus also used exaggerated language in order to create a greater impression and to stir his hearers to reflect upon the reality which he was teaching. Again numerous examples are available. "It is easier for a camel to go through the eye of a needle than for a rich man to enter the kingdom of God" (MARK 10:25) by its exaggerated language challenges anyone with possessions to reflect seriously upon his relationship with God and the danger of the love of money (1 Tim. 6:10). Calling the scribes and Pharisees hypocrites because they strain out gnats but swallow camels (Matt. 23:24) is clearly hyperbolic.[3] While the figure is impossible, it is a striking and unforgettable picture of the behavior of the scribes and Pharisees. Similarly, the warning to take the log out of one's own eye before seeking to remove the speck from a brother's (MATT. 7:5) is a vivid portrayal of the hypocrisy involved in judging the faults of others while ignoring one's own.

The value of exaggerated language

At times exaggeration serves a most useful function in speech and literature. It frequently has great mnemonic value since it creates a picture that is unforgettable. Who can forget the figures of a speck in one eye and a log in another, a camel going through the eye of a needle, straining gnats and swallowing camels? Such pictures are long remembered. No doubt Jesus intended such language to aid his hearers in remembering what he taught, for without access to pencil and paper or cassette recorders the vast majority of his audience had no means of preserving what he taught other than to memorize his words. The use of exaggeration made the task of remembering easier.

Another valuable function of exaggerated language is that it facilitates decision and change by impressing upon the hearer the seriousness of what the speaker is teaching. LUKE 14:26 teaches that following Jesus does not involve some cheap and easy faith; rather, it involves hating one's parents! Following Jesus is not, as Dietrich Bonhoeffer pointed out, a "cheap grace." No, it involves placing Jesus before all else. The many woes pronounced upon the Pharisees and scribes in Matthew 23 use harsh exaggeration (note the universal condemnation of all the Pharisees and scribes—they make proselytes children of hell [v. 15]; they strain out gnats but swallow camels [v. 24]; they are full of extortion and rapacity [v. 25]) and various graphic similes and metaphors (like whitewashed tombs [v. 27]; serpents, brood of vipers [v. 33]) in order to emphasize the gravity of their hypocrisy and the need to repent and change. In this way exaggeration functions in literature much as does verbal intonation in speech. A soft, mild "Watch out!" does not in any way affect the hearer as does a "WATCH OUT!" screamed as loudly as possible. Exaggerated language can serve as a scream of warning to bring the hearer's attention to the subject at hand and facilitate the appropriate response. Exaggeration is far more forceful and compelling in this regard than any literal statement can ever be.

A third purpose for the use of exaggerated language is to help communicate exactly how the speaker feels concerning the issue at hand. The psalmist revealed by his use of exaggeration his great love for the city of Jerusalem:

> His holy mountain,, beautiful in elevation, is the joy of all the earth. [48:1-2]

> If I forget you, O Jerusalem, let my right hand wither! Let my tongue cleave to the roof of my mouth, if I do not remember you, if I do not set Jerusalem above my highest joy! [137:5-6]

In like manner Jesus frequently revealed his innermost feelings by the use of exaggerated language. Note how the following examples enable us to catch a glimpse of his deepest emotions. When asked for his essential thoughts on the matter of divorce, he replied:

> Whoever divorces his wife and marries another, commits adultery against her; and if she divorces her husband and marries another, she commits adultery. [MARK 10:11-12]

Having decried the use of prayer as a means of gaining public applause and recognition, he enjoined:

> But when you pray, go into your room and shut the door and pray to your Father who is in secret; and your Father who sees in secret will reward you. [Matt. 6:6]

And having denounced those who fasted in order to be seen and admired by others, and not in order to please God, he taught:·

But when you fast, anoint your head and wash your face,
that your fasting may not be seen by men but by your Father
who is in secret; and your Father who sees in secret will
reward you. [Matt. 6:17-18]

Finally, as he faced the agony of the cross he said, "My soul
is very sorrowful, even to death" [MARK 14:34]. Perhaps
nowhere do we feel the heartbeat of Jesus more fully than
we feel it in his use of exaggerated language.[4]

A final function of exaggeration in language is to stimulate
our interest and hold our attention. Exaggeration makes one
sit up and take notice. Literal language unbroken by metaphor or exaggeration tends to be monotonous or at least
dull, but hyperbole or overstatement creates a certain ten-
sion which awakens not only the interest of the hearer but
also his thinking process. It teases the hearer into wrestling
with the underlying meaning of what is being said. Because
exaggerations contradict our ordinary way of thinking, they
raise questions. The greater the exaggeration, the more we
are challenged to arrive at the real intention of the author
or speaker: What exactly does he mean? Can he really expect
us to understand him literally, to carry out his instructions
to the letter? If not, what is he driving at? Needless to say,
this attention-getting purpose of exaggeration may be present in combination with its mnemonic, performative, and
expressive purposes. Use of exaggeration for one purpose
does not automatically exclude the others.

Notes

1. The writer is indebted to G. B. Caird, *The Language and Imagery of
the Bible* (Philadelphia: Westminster, 1980), pp. 7–36, for much of the
terminology used in this section. Caird subdivides referential language
into informative and cognitive language, and commissive language into
performative, expressive, and cohesive language.

2. Philip Wheelwright, *Metaphor and Reality* (Bloomington: Indiana
University Press, 1962), p. 38.

3. There is also a pun here—the Aramaic word for gnat was *galma* and
for camel was *gamla*. See Robert H. Stein, *The Method and Message of Jesus'
Teaching* (Philadelphia: Westminster, 1978), p. 13.

4. Claude C. Douglas, *Overstatement in the New Testament* (New York:

Henry Holt, 1931), p. 3, states, "In general hyperbole increases in proportion to the intensity of the emotion experienced by the speaker or writer."

Conclusion

We have noted a number of reasons why Jesus chose to use exaggerated language in his teachings. It must be pointed out here that he never did so in order to deceive. The doctoring of business ledgers, so that the assets look greater than they really are, and the distorting of facts by a totalitarian state are not legitimate uses of exaggerated language. Jesus always assumed that his readers, either through intuition or logic, would understand that exaggeration was being used and would interpret his sayings accordingly. Exaggeration is a legitimate device in speech or literature only if the audience recognizes it as such. In most instances this is no major problem. But in our scientific age it is important to remind ourselves that Jesus frequently made use of the picturesque language of metaphor and exaggeration. As a result, we must take care to understand not merely the lexical meaning of Jesus' words, but also the underlying intent in his particular use of these figures of speech. This is a most important step in interpreting the teachings of Jesus, for in such passages the language used does not always correspond with the intended meaning. We must be careful to distinguish between the *referent* of a verbal symbol, that is, the object to which it literally refers, and the *sense*, that is, the mental image the verbal symbol is intended to convey.

More often than not, our intuition will keep us from interpreting Jesus' metaphors and exaggerations literally. This is especially true if we are well acquainted with the teachings of Jesus in general. The canons which have been listed in chapter 2 can serve as additional tools in the hermeneutical process. While they will not always enable us to determine with absolute certainty whether a saying is an exaggeration, they will allow us nevertheless to base our interpretation on more than intuition.

Recognition that a particular text contains exaggeration, however, does not end the hermeneutical process. Having noted the presence of exaggeration, we must seek to understand why Jesus used exaggeration in this particular instance. That an exaggeration which occurs in a command is performative in function is readily apparent. In such cases Jesus was emphatically seeking to bring about a decision of some sort. But we must also determine the precise decision expected of the original audience (the first *Sitz im Leben*), the original readers of the Gospel (the third *Sitz im Leben*), and the present reader as well. Furthermore, we must bear in mind that the presence of exaggeration in the teachings of Jesus in no way lessens the radical nature of their demand. To interpret LUKE 14:26 to mean not that we should hate our parents, but that love for Christ must take precedence over all human love, even the love of a husband for a wife or of parents for their children, does not lessen the radical nature of the demand at all. Abraham knew this (Gen. 22)! Likewise repentance, correctly understood, is even a more radical demand than the plucking out of an eye or the cutting off of a hand (MARK 9:43–47), for it involves a fundamental change of the entire person, not simply the violent removal of one part of the body!

Due to the present abundance of writing materials, the mnemonic value of exaggeration may not be as important today as in Jesus' day. The attention-getting purpose of an exaggeration may also be less important today for some; but the expressive purpose of such sayings is still very significant, for they reveal Jesus' innermost feelings on vital issues. While all the teachings of Jesus are important for the Christian, Jesus used exaggeration to highlight those to which he wanted to give additional emphasis. It is therefore incumbent on the Christian reader today to give special attention to and scrupulously heed those teachings.

Scripture Index

Genesis

1—71
11:4—85
13:16—83-84
15:5—84
22—100
22:17—35, 79
24:60—85
29:30-31—77-78
32:12—79, 84
48:17-20—42

Exodus

1:7-9—85
3:7-8—84
3:17—84
14:21-29—70
14:23—70
14:26-28—70
15—70
15:1—70
15:3—70
15:4—70
15:7—70
15:8-10—70
15:21—70
20:7—45
20:12—45
20:13—25

Leviticus

5:1—43, 45
19:3—45

19:12—45
19:18—44

Numbers

10:36—85
30:2-15—45

Deuteronomy

1:8—45
1:28—85
5:16—45
6:5—44
21:15-17—77
23:21-23—45
24:1—49
28:25-46—62
28:39—86

Joshua

2:11—78
5:1—78
7:5—78
11:4—79

Judges

4—69
4:21—87
5:4-5—69-70
5:19-20—69-70
5:26—87
7:12—79, 85
20:16—85

1 Samuel

2:12—58
8:5—58

2 Samuel

1:23—35, 85
12:1-4—73
17:10—78
19:6—77
22:8-16—70

1 Kings

21:20-29—61
22:16—43

Job

6:2-4—83
7:5-6—83
9:17-18—83
16:9—80
16:11-16—83
38:7—35

Psalms

2:1-2—66
3:6—85
6:6-7—83
19:1-4—35
22—83
22:6—72
35:16—80

37:12—80
38—83
48:1-2—95
69—83
88:3-9—83
102:3-11—72, 83
104—71
110:4—45
112:10—78, 80
132:11—45
137:5-6—95
137:8-9—78
139—24
144:13—85

Proverbs

3:9-10—57-58
10:1—45
10:3-4—57-58
13:21—57-58
13:24—77
14:30—69
15:1—57-58
15:20—45, 69
17:2—57-58
22:6—58
22:16—58
23:22—45
29:24—43

Song of Solomon

2:1—72